# FARRAGUT NORTH

# NORTH

BY **BEAU WILLIMON**

★

★

DRAMATISTS
PLAY SERVICE
INC.

FARRAGUT NORTH
Copyright © 2009, Beau Willimon

All Rights Reserved

FARRAGUT NORTH was given its World Premiere by Atlantic Theater Company (Neil Pepe, Artistic Director; Andrew D. Hamingson, Managing Director; Christian Parker, Associate Artistic Director) in New York City at the Linda Gross Theater on November 12, 2008. It was directed by Doug Hughes; the assistant director was David Ruttura; the fight director was J. David Brimmer; the set design was by David Korins; the costume design was by Catherine Zuber; the lighting design was by Paul Gallo; the original music was by David Van Tieghem; the sound design was by David Van Tieghem and Walter Trarbach; the projections were by Joshua White; the production stage manager was Barclay Stiff; the production manager was Michael Wade; and the casting was by Telsey + Company. The cast was as follows:

BEN ........................................................................ Dan Bittner
IDA ..................................................................... Kate Blumberg
STEPHEN ...................................................... John Gallagher, Jr.
PAUL ...................................................................... Chris Noth
WAITER/FRANK ................................................. Otto Sanchez
MOLLY ............................................................ Olivia Thirlby
TOM ............................................................ Isiah Whitlock, Jr.

# CHARACTERS

STEPHEN BELLAMY — 25, press secretary for presidential candidate Governor Morris

PAUL ZARA — late 40s, campaign manager for Governor Morris

MOLLY — 19, an intern on the Morris campaign

BEN — early 20s, deputy press secretary for the Morris campaign

TOM DUFFY — late 40s – early 50s, campaign manager for the rival Pullman campaign

IDA HOROWICZ — mid-30s, a traveling political reporter for *The New York Times*

FRANK — a reporter for the *Los Angeles Times*

WAITER (can be played by the same actor who plays FRANK)

# SETTING

## ACT ONE

Scene 1: January. The bar of the Hotel Fort Des Moines, Des Moines, Iowa.

Scene 2: Later that evening at a small, dingy restaurant in East Des Moines.

Scene 3: Early the next morning in Stephen's hotel room.

Scene 4: Later that morning, the Des Moines airport.

## ACT TWO

Scene 1: Later that afternoon at a campaign event in Cedar Rapids, Iowa.

Scene 2: A few hours later, Molly's office at the campaign headquarters in Des Moines.

Scene 3: Later that evening, Paul's room at the Hotel Fort Des Moines.

Scene 4: An hour later at the same dingy restaurant as Act One.

Scene 5: Late that night, Stephen's room at the Hotel Fort Des Moines.

NOTE: A backslash ( / ) indicates where the following line is meant to begin overlapping the current one.

# FARRAGUT NORTH

## ACT ONE

### Scene 1

*January. Early evening. The bar of the Hotel Fort Des Moines. The décor is faux opulent. Paul, Ida, Ben and Stephen sit at a table, drinking. Paul has a roll-away suitcase beside him.*

STEPHEN.  I played you. Like a fucking fiddle.

IDA.  Now Stevie …

STEPHEN.  It's true.

IDA.  You didn't / *play* me.

STEPHEN.  Like a well-tuned fiddle.

IDA.  *(To Paul.)* It was the first race I ever covered.

STEPHEN.  She was gullible.

IDA.  *(Flicking him off.)* You see this?

STEPHEN.  Putty in / my —

IDA.  *(To Stephen.)* You didn't play me, you *convinced* me. You *persuaded* me. There's a difference. I knew exactly / what I was doing.

PAUL.  *(To Stephen.)* Come on, come on. Back to the story.

STEPHEN.  Right. So this was what — '04?

BEN.  '02.

STEPHEN.  '02. Thank you, Ben.

BEN.  We studied *Cabrisi vs. Goldman* in one of our poli sci classes.

STEPHEN.  No shit?

BEN.  Yeah. I even wrote a paper on it.

STEPHEN.  There ya go — I'm already a footnote in history.

BEN.  Well, it's not like the paper was published or anything. I mean the only person who read it was / the —

STEPHEN. *(Cutting him off.)* So right, this was '02.

PAUL. You were … Jesus … you were twenty. I keep forgetting that.

STEPHEN. Just turned twenty. My third — no — my fourth campaign.

PAUL. Twenty fucking years old.

IDA. We couldn't even buy him drinks.

STEPHEN. I managed to sneak my fair share.

IDA. You managed to sneak *more* than your fair share.

PAUL. So the race …

STEPHEN. The race. Tight, tight fucking race. And this was New York politics — *nasty.* Just as rough and tumble as anything you see out here in Des Moines.

IDA. But not as cold.

STEPHEN. Fuckin' Iowa.

IDA. I can't wait until Florida.

PAUL. Come on, come on.

STEPHEN. Okay … so ten days out, our internals show the suburbs are slipping. Point and a half, two points a day. Now this slides out of the margin and we're fucked. Papers will show Cabrisi with the momentum. On top of it all, the press is pounding the shit out of us. Hit after hit after hit. Including you, Ida. You were the worst of 'em.

IDA. I was just being a responsible journalist.

STEPHEN. You were being a bitch.

IDA. I was being a little bit of a bitch. Not as bad as Gordon, or Judy, at the *Post.* Judy was the *real* bitch.

STEPHEN. You were better than Judy, that's true.

PAUL. So …

STEPHEN. So yeah. I'm thinking — okay, it's over. Chalk this one up and move on. Can't win 'em all. *Then* — Then a miracle drops in our lap.

IDA. Cabrisi's people should have just locked him up in a padded room. He had it in the bag.

STEPHEN. The fucking bag. It was his to lose.

BEN. You're talking about that comment, right — that thing Cabrisi / called —

STEPHEN. Who's telling this story Ben?

BEN. I'm sorry, I …

PAUL. So the miracle.

STEPHEN. Like manna from the heavens. Cabrisi's at this fundraiser out in Flatbush, raising cash from all the conservative Jews that hate Goldman. Starts ripping on Goldman, joking around, playing the crowd. At one point, he calls Goldman a *putzhead*. Gets a laugh, moves on. Nobody thinks twice about it.

IDA. But there's this AP reporter there.

STEPHEN. Total lightweight.

IDA. Josh Carlin, local beat guy.

STEPHEN. He's a big shot now. Covering the West Bank or some shit like that …

PAUL. Keep going; I wanna get to the good part.

STEPHEN. Well Josh, right, he throws this blurb on the wire. Little thing. Headline was something like "Cabrisi Gives Remarks at Flatbush Fundraiser." Doesn't make a ripple. But our oppo guys, they read this blurb and they rush over to my office. "Look! Look! Carbrisi called Goldman a putzhead!" And I'm like "So what? Who cares? So he called him a putzhead — he's called us worse." And they're like — no, this is big. Apparently putzhead is Yiddish for dickhead. Meaning, Cabrisi publicly called Goldman a *dickhead* in Yiddish.

PAUL. *(Laughing.)* I love it.

STEPHEN. Beautiful, right?

PAUL. You have your silver bullet.

STEPHEN. Exactly. So now I gotta figure out how to spin this. Problem is, *we* can't send out a release. It'll look like some desperate attack. So what I *do* / is —

IDA. This was brilliant, I have to admit.

STEPHEN. What I do is, I call up the president of the Democratic Jewish League — big supporter — threw us lots of money — and I read this AP story to him. Name was Mencken …

PAUL. Harvey Mencken — I know him.

STEPHEN. Right. So I say, *Harvey* — we've got a great opportunity to fuck Cabrisi here. I want you to send out a release quoting this putzhead comment and accusing Cabrisi of anti-Semitism. He jumps at it. I dictate the whole release to him over the phone, it's out in fifteen minutes. Then I have Harvey organize a press conference with prominent Jewish leaders all denouncing Cabrisi as an anti-Semite, which he does.

PAUL. Gorgeous.

STEPHEN. That's what I thought, but it doesn't stick. I make a few calls but the reporters aren't biting, and I don't want to seem aggressive or it would look like I orchestrated it all.

IDA. Which you did.

STEPHEN. But that's not what I want them to think. So I'm like — fuck — how do I get this out there? What's the one place where — if I can get this to land — the one place that will force everyone else to jump on board?

PAUL. The *Times*.

STEPHEN. Bingo. So I give *Ida* a call.

IDA. And he used this sweet little innocent voice, like all of this was news to him.

STEPHEN. She didn't want to print it. Thought the story "unworthy" of the *Times*.

PAUL. So of course you worked your magic.

IDA. He made me a wager.

STEPHEN. What I say is — "Ida, off the record, let's be straight here. You've been fucking us over for the past two weeks and giving Cabrisi a total pass. You owe us. And if you write this story, I guarantee you — I fucking *guarantee* you that your editors will put it on the front page."

IDA. To which I said, "Bullshit."

STEPHEN. So I say, "Look — if your editors don't put this story on the front page not only will I buy you dinner at any restaurant of your choice in the city, but I will quit my job and never work in politics again. If it *does* make it on the front page you've got your first front page byline and I'll still buy you dinner."

PAUL. *(To Ida.)* So you wrote the story.

IDA. I did.

STEPHEN. And not only did it make it on the front page of the *Times*, it got two columns *above* the fucking fold.

IDA. "Cabrisi Accused of Anti-Semitism" by Ida Horowicz.

STEPHEN. It was an avalanche. Cabrisi's on the defensive, first denying the remark, then admitting to it, then refusing to apologize, then *forced* to apologize. Within one news cycle, the story was being covered by every TV, radio station and newspaper in New York State. It's running non-stop on all the twenty-four-hour news channels. Overnight Cabrisi drops ten points. His message gets drowned out. Four days later we win by twelve. Total blowout.

PAUL. Beautiful. *(To Ben.)* You should keep an eye on Stevie, you'll learn everything you need to know.

STEPHEN.  Ben's twice as smart as I'll ever be.

BEN.  Yeah, right.

STEPHEN.  I'm getting old, I'll have to pass the torch eventually.

IDA.  A wizened twenty-five. You'll need a wheelchair before too long.

PAUL.  I still can't believe Goldman hired a fucking twenty-year-old for his press secretary.

IDA.  I can't believe that Morris hired a *twenty-five-year-old*. A Senate race is one thing, but a presidential...?

STEPHEN.  Hey — I'm keepin' my head above the water.

PAUL.  *(To Stephen.)* You're doing more than that. *(To Ida.)* When I told the Governor I wanted to hire Stevie. He said to me, "Paul — hire that fuckin' kid before somebody else does."

IDA.  And look where he is now.

PAUL.  Doing *my* dirty work.

IDA.  God help us.

BEN.  Does anyone else need a refill?

IDA.  I'm good.

STEPHEN.  Come on, Ida, have another.

IDA.  Tempting, but no.

BEN.  Paul?

PAUL.  *(Looking at his watch.)* I'd love another, but I gotta get going in a few. Goddamn security at the airport. Speaking of which, I should call a cab.

IDA.  You want me to drive you?

PAUL.  You have a car?

IDA.  A rental. Yeah. A Suburban, no less.

PAUL.  Four-wheel-drive?

IDA.  Anti-lock brakes, airbags — the works.

PAUL.  Well then, hell — sure — I'll take a lift. *(To Ben.)* And I'll take another Jack and Coke. *(Looking at his watch.)* Still got a few minutes.

BEN.  Steve?

STEVE.  I'll take a —

PAUL.  No more for Stevie. *(To Stephen.)* You've got that press conference.

STEPHEN.  *(To Ben.)* I'm fine.

BEN.  One Jack and Coke then. *(Ben exits.)*

PAUL.  He's a good kid. Got a lot to learn, but a good kid.

STEPHEN.  Definitely worth keeping an eye on.

IDA. So, Paul …

PAUL. Yes, Ida?

IDA. Paul, Paul, Paul …

PAUL. Here it comes. *(To Stephen.)* When she gets that shit-eating grin on her face, I know she wants something. *(To Ida.)* Hit me.

IDA. You're going to the airport.

PAUL. Yes?

IDA. You're getting on a plane.

PAUL. Mm-hmm.

IDA. Where is that plane going?

PAUL. *(To Stephen.)* You see?

IDA. Out with it.

PAUL. Three guesses.

IDA. You're not going back to headquarters.

PAUL. Correct.

IDA. You're not going to New Hampshire.

PAUL. *(To Stephen.)* Look at these deductive skills we got goin' on here.

IDA. What if I said South Carolina?

PAUL. That's your final answer?

IDA. Final answer. You're going to South Carolina.

PAUL. I will neither confirm nor deny that statement.

IDA. I knew it.

STEPHEN. She's on fire.

IDA. Now tell me why.

PAUL. That I cannot do.

IDA. Pretty please?

PAUL. No.

IDA. A hint.

PAUL. Not a chance.

IDA. Nothing?

PAUL. Nada.

IDA. I hate you.

PAUL. You love me.

IDA. I love Stevie. You, I hate.

STEPHEN. You only love me because I give you all the scoops.

IDA. Well, I deserve to be wooed.

STEPHEN. And because I got Paul to agree to your profile.

PAUL. Which wasn't easy, by the way.

IDA. You don't relish spending every living moment together?

PAUL.  Maybe if you weren't constantly trying to bait me.

IDA.  Wouldn't be a very good profile then, would it?

PAUL.  Probably won't be anyway.

STEPHEN.  She'll make it nice, won't you, Ida?

IDA.  No promises, my dear.

PAUL.  It better be good. I've given you great stuff.

IDA.  Heavy drinking, chewing tobacco, lewd comments … yeah — I'd say so.

PAUL.  You drink more than I do.

IDA.  But the profile's not about me. And I don't chew tobacco.

PAUL.  "Paul Zara Has Flaws" — there's your headline.

IDA.  Or maybe something like: "Morris's Campaign Manager: Barbarian at the Gate."

PAUL.  You should do a profile on Stevie here. He's more interesting than I am.

IDA.  But he doesn't have any flaws.

STEPHEN.  Flattery won't get you shit.

IDA.  Sexual favors?

STEPHEN.  You're engaged.

IDA.  If it meant a good story, my fiancé would understand.

PAUL.  So it's gonna be one of those marriages, huh?

IDA.  You think I'd let any husband of *mine* wear the pants?

STEPHEN.  Let me see that rock again. *(Ida shows him a ring.)* Unbelievable.

IDA.  Nice, huh?

PAUL.  At least you're marrying rich.

IDA.  Is there any other way?

STEPHEN.  Let's go to a pawn shop and hock this thing. We'll get tickets to Vegas and get hitched at some tacky twenty-four-hour chapel.

IDA.  In your dreams.

STEPHEN.  You're breaking my heart.

IDA.  You two are breaking my heart by not telling me what this South Carolina thing is about.

PAUL.  Poor baby.

IDA.  *(To Paul.)* How's Mrs. Zara by the way?

PAUL.  Mrs. Zara? She's miserable. Just like she always is. Other than that, she's great.

IDA.  *(To Stephen.)* And Steve — how's Helen?

PAUL.  Kaput.

IDA. What?

PAUL. Bye-bye, Helen.

IDA. Really?!

STEPHEN. Not kaput, necessarily, just …

PAUL. It's over.

IDA. No!

PAUL. Done. Finis.

STEPHEN. It's really not a big deal.

IDA. It's over between you guys?

STEPHEN. Kind of — for now — yes.

IDA. When?!

STEPHEN. Week or two ago.

PAUL. Stevie's a free man.

IDA. I'm so sorry.

STEPHEN. Really, it's not a big deal. We're just … just taking a break, you know?

PAUL. Sure you are.

IDA. A little sensitivity is in order here, Paul.

PAUL. It's for the best. *(To Stephen.)* You wouldn't have time for her once you got to the White House anyway.

IDA. *(To Stephen.)* So what happened?

STEPHEN. It's not even worth getting into. Really. Let's change the subject. We're having drinks. We're ahead in the polls. These are happy times, right?

PAUL. Don't worry about him, Ida. This boy is bulletproof. *(Ben returns with Paul's drink.)*

BEN. Here you go.

PAUL. How much do I owe you?

BEN. I got it.

PAUL. Fuck off. You don't get paid well enough to buy me a drink. How much?

BEN. Really. I got it.

PAUL. *(To Stephen.)* I'm telling you — he's a good kid. *(Raising his glass.)* To happy times.

STEPHEN. To happy times. *(They all clink glasses, except for Ben.)*

IDA. So, changing the subject. Paul — tell me something I don't know.

PAUL. You know everything.

IDA. I don't know why you're going to South Carolina.

PAUL. That wasn't changing the subject.

IDA. Fine. Tell me what's gonna happen on the nineteenth.

PAUL. Haha.

IDA. What?

PAUL. What do you think, Stevie?

STEPHEN. It's ours for the taking.

PAUL. Ben?

BEN. We'll win.

PAUL. What do you think, Ida?

IDA. I'm asking *you.*

PAUL. You tell me and I'll tell you.

IDA. If I had to say, I'd say it'll be close, but you'll eke it out.

PAUL. Eke? We'll *eke* it out? *(To Stephen.)* You see, she's trying to get under my skin.

IDA. So what's gonna happen?

PAUL. Us by nine.

IDA. *Nine?* There's no way you'll win by nine.

STEPHEN. At least. Maybe more.

IDA. Sounds pretty optimistic to me.

PAUL. You don't get into this game if you're a pessimist.

IDA. You don't *win* unless you're a realist.

STEPHEN. We'll win Iowa by nine. Ogelby drops because he tanks here. Even if Pullman picks up his people, we'll take New Hampshire by double digits. Morris jumps out on the twenty-seventh with enough momentum to take no less than five of seven on Super Tuesday, maybe even a clean sweep.

IDA. South Carolina?

STEPHEN. We can take it.

IDA. Doubtful.

STEPHEN. Even if we don't — we take five or six of the seven, and it's over. Pullman runs dry on cash, the Party rallies behind us, we got three weeks to hammer Pullman into the dust before the next big round.

IDA. You got it all planned out.

PAUL. Listen to the boy — he knows what he's talking about.

IDA. *(To Paul.)* So you're certain you're gonna win here?

PAUL. *Certain?* No. Confident? Yes.

IDA. You just said you'll win by nine.

PAUL. And I think we will, but I won't tell you it's a sure thing. Saint Gabriel could blow his fuckin' horn on election day and get his four horseman to rig the ballot boxes for Pullman, and it

15

wouldn't surprise me. Don't get me wrong. Six presidentials I've done and I've never felt this good. But am I gonna sit here and say "Yes — Morris will definitely win Iowa"? Not a chance. In the last thirty years seventy-one Democrats have run for president. How many have won? Two. That means sixty-nine people ran who thought they had a chance, and they all lost. Nobody on this planet knows how to win a presidential campaign. Not Pullman, not Ogelby, not Morris — no one.

IDA. So you're saying there's a good chance you'll lose.

PAUL. What I'm saying is that I won't *promise* we'll win. But — okay now. If we *do* win, if we *do* take Iowa —

IDA. You *have* to take Iowa.

PAUL. You're damn straight we do. Morris not only has to win Iowa — he needs to *crush* Pullman. And I think we can. And when we do — our internet support will go through the roof. We'll hit two million supporters by July. At two million, we'll hit a boiling point. Every motherfucker that's felt beaten and bullied and busted by the powers that be is gonna suddenly realize — hey, we can stick it to the Man here. We can take on big business, oil, drug companies. Two million will become three million, then four, then five. We have the potential to raise *half a billion dollars*. The grass-roots will become the mainstream. The mainstream will water the lawn, and that lawn will stretch from Maine to New Mexico, from Alaska to Florida. I don't use the word revolution lightly, but that's what this could be. Millions of people standing up and saying "This is *our* goddamn country — We're gonna take it back from those who have stolen it from us. We're gonna make the impossible *possible* again." And on *that* note, I'm gonna go take a shit before I get on this plane. *(Paul swigs down the rest of his drink and exits.)*

IDA. He's crazy.

STEPHEN. He's a genius.

IDA. Do you really buy into all that crap? All that take-back-the-country nonsense?

STEPHEN. Buy into it? I believe that everything Paul says is *possible*. If there was ever a time a campaign like ours, that an insurgent with a real message was gonna — yeah. I guess I do. I do buy into it.

IDA. Half a billion dollars?

STEPHEN. Six months ago who would have thought we'd raised fifty by now?

IDA.  That's a long ways from five hundred.

STEPHEN.  Six months ago Morris was a nobody. Now we're leading the polls. You know me — I'm not naïve about this stuff. I've worked on more campaigns than most people do by the time they're forty. This is the one, Ida.

IDA.  You really *have* drunk the Kool-Aid.

STEPHEN.  It's good. You should try some.

IDA.  What about you, Ben?

BEN.  Everything Steve just said.

IDA.  Ha-ha. You've trained him well.

STEPHEN.  I'm not shitting you here, Ida. This is it. I've had a good dose of cynicism pumped into me with every campaign I've worked on. But this thing, it's got me starry-eyed again. It's reminded me why I got into politics in the first place. I mean, look — I grew up in a shit stain by the side of the road fifty miles south of D.C., but it might as well have been fifty thousand. Half the folks in my town didn't even know the word "congress" has two S's in it, much less who their congressman was. I made my way to D.C., race by race — traded in my accent for this fucking crackberry. And why? Because I didn't want to drive a tractor for the rest of my life. I wanted to be something. I wanted to change the world. That's what I love about my job. Every day is a chance to make a real difference.

IDA.  *(To Ben.)* Get out of this business now or you'll start sounding like Steve.

STEPHEN.  Don't listen to her. She gets paid to spoil the fun.

IDA.  Not paid well.

STEPHEN.  Better than I do.

IDA.  You get power, prestige and the chance to change history. I get my name printed in eight point on cheap news-stock. I deserve a few extra bucks for my troubles. *(Paul returns and sits.)*

PAUL.  No dice. I'm constipated.

STEPHEN.  Ouch.

PAUL.  Heaved and huffed on the can but zilch — nothing came out. 'Cept some rabbit pellets. Mother lode's still stuck up in there somewhere.

IDA.  Thanks, Paul. I'll try to erase that image from my mind while I drive you to the airport.

PAUL.  Too many carbs. Always happens. I oughtta go on one of those protein diets.

STEPHEN. You can shit properly *and* lose weight at the same time.

PAUL. You saying I'm fat? *(He stuffs a wad of chewing tobacco into his mouth.)*

STEPHEN. I wouldn't say you're skinny.

PAUL. What do you think, Ben? You think I'm fat?

BEN. No. Not at all.

PAUL. Ass-kisser. I *am* getting fat. And it looks even worse 'cause I'm bloated at the moment.

IDA. Stop it.

PAUL. *(To Ida.)* You know — the only reason I chew this stuff is because it's a diuretic.

IDA. Speaking of which, I'm actually gonna hit the john before we head out. Be right back. *(She exits. Paul hands Ben a few dollars.)*

PAUL. Ben, go get yourself a drink. I owe you one.

BEN. That's okay, I'm not really —

PAUL. Go get yourself a drink.

BEN. Seriously, I'm fine.

PAUL. I don't think you're hearing me. I'm saying you should take this money and go get yourself a drink.

BEN. Oh. Right. *(Ben takes the money and exits.)*

PAUL. Whatta ya think?

STEPHEN. I leak it to her. Nothing specific, just enough to whet her appetite.

PAUL. She'll hound me on the drive to the airport.

STEPHEN. No she won't. I leak it like you don't know, on the condition she keeps it quiet.

PAUL. You really think she will?

STEPHEN. She owes me. I got her this profile with you, and she'll owe me double if I give her this leak off the record.

PAUL. I don't know.

STEPHEN. She just wants to feel like she's in the loop. If I give her this off the record now, she'll write a terrific story once we go public. We keep it secret, she'll fuck us.

PAUL. How? There's no way you can turn this into a bad story.

STEPHEN. Ida can always find a way.

PAUL. No specifics.

STEPHEN. I'll keep it vague.

PAUL. 'Cause if it gets out, the whole thing could fold.

STEPHEN. I know what I'm doing.

PAUL. I know you know what you're doing. I just get a little, you know …

STEPHEN. This is the best way to go.

PAUL. Alright, Steve. Alright. If you say this is the way to go, then this is the way to go.

STEPHEN. I've never let you down, have I?

PAUL. Not yet.

STEPHEN. Come on.

PAUL. I trust you. So do your thing. Leak it. Make it nice.

STEPHEN. Done.

PAUL. Now as for this press conference tonight …

STEPHEN. I've got it under control.

PAUL. They're gonna try to hit us on the new poll numbers.

STEPHEN. As long as the Governor keeps to my talking points, we should be fine. And this white paper, Paul — it's good. Gonna nail Pullman on renewable energy with a hammer *this* big.

PAUL. Don't know what I'd do without you, Stevie.

STEPHEN. How about a raise?

PAUL. You'll get your raise once we make it to the White House. *(Ida returns.)*

STEPHEN. That was quick.

IDA. I don't have the same problems Paul does.

PAUL. Watch it — I'll shit in your Suburban.

IDA. That'd make a story.

PAUL. *(Looking at his watch.)* We should get going.

IDA. I'll pull up out front.

PAUL. Gimme the keys, I'll pick *you* up.

IDA. Not a chance.

PAUL. Gimme the goddamned keys. I haven't driven a car in months. And I *looooove* driving in the snow. *(Ida hands him the keys.)*

IDA. It's in the garage across the street. Second floor.

PAUL. *(Taking the keys. To Stephen.)* You behave yourself.

STEPHEN. Always.

PAUL. *(To Ida.)* I'll see you out front. *(Paul exits with his suitcase. During the following conversation, Molly enters, carrying a manila envelope. Seeing that Stephen is talking to Ida, she hangs off to the side, waiting for them to finish up so as not to interrupt.)*

IDA. He's gonna crash my rental, isn't he?

STEPHEN. Probably.

IDA. I should have ordered a second drink.

STEPHEN. Thompson.

IDA. What?

STEPHEN. Marcellus Thompson.

IDA. Seriously?

STEPHEN. This is off off *off* the record. You can't let Paul have the slightest idea you know or it'll be my ass. The only people who know are the Governor, Paul and me.

IDA. My lips are sealed.

STEPHEN. They have a meeting tomorrow at Thompson's house.

IDA. He's gonna endorse?

STEPHEN. After Paul's done talking with him, what do you think?

IDA. That's huge.

STEPHEN. It's more than huge. We'll lock up half the black vote in South Carolina overnight once this comes out.

IDA. He's said publicly he's not gonna endorse anyone.

STEPHEN. That's what they all say until we get them alone in a room.

IDA. So this is for real?

STEPHEN. Yup.

IDA. For *real* real?

STEPHEN. Just about in the bag.

IDA. When are you gonna announce?

STEPHEN. Nope. That's all you get for now.

IDA. You'll give me the scoop, right?

STEPHEN. Maybe. If you're nice.

IDA. I want that story.

STEPHEN. Sure you do. So you play nice, and we'll play nice.

IDA. Let's talk after the press conference. I'll do my best to keep an open mind if you're trying to push anything, keeping my journalistic standards intact, of course.

STEPHEN. Of course.

IDA. You're the best, Stevie. I'll talk to you later. *(Ida exits. Stephen immediately grabs his phone and begins to dial. Molly approaches Stephen, standing behind him while he makes his phone call.)*

STEPHEN. Paul? It's done … yeah … Easy as pie. *(Laughs.)* Okay, you too. Good luck out there. *(He hangs up.)*

MOLLY. Steve?

STEPHEN. *(Startled.)* Oh um … uh … Mary?

MOLLY. Molly.

STEPHEN.  Right right right — Molly.

MOLLY.  I worked at headquarters.

STEPHEN.  No — I remember.

MOLLY.  Yeah.

STEPHEN.  Scared the shit out of me.

MOLLY.  Sorry … I … —

STEPHEN.  What are you doing out in Iowa?

MOLLY.  I volunteered to come out here a few days ago.

STEPHEN.  That's great.

MOLLY.  Yeah, I was getting sick of headquarters. It's so dead there now. Everybody's out here.

STEPHEN.  What do they have you doing?

MOLLY.  Same stuff. Blogging mostly. Filling gaps where they can use me.

STEPHEN.  Very cool. *(Molly holds out the envelope.)*

MOLLY.  Anyway — this is for you. The folks in the press shop said you'd be here.

STEPHEN.  Oh, right. Thanks. I've been waiting for this.

MOLLY.  Anything interesting?

STEPHEN.  *(Mock-serious.)* Top secret.

MOLLY.  Gotcha.

STEPHEN.  Just some white paper I gotta pass out tonight.

MOLLY.  White paper?

STEPHEN.  Negative shit. Our oppo guys do research — we feed it to the press, hope they bite.

MOLLY.  So like what sort of negative stuff?

STEPHEN.  Read tomorrow's paper and you'll see.

MOLLY.  Which paper?

STEPHEN.  All of them.

MOLLY.  So it's something big?

STEPHEN.  I wish it were something bigger actually. Just some renewable energy figures. I'll have to spin this shit pretty heavy if we want it to stick.

MOLLY.  Well, that's what you're good at, right? Spinning things …

STEPHEN.  I guess.

MOLLY.  Anyway … it was good seeing you. Good luck at the press conference. *(She starts to go.)*

STEPHEN.  Hey, Molly? Sorry for getting your name wrong.

MOLLY.  Oh — that's okay.

STEPHEN.  No, it's not. We worked in the same office for what

— two, three months. I should know your name.

MOLLY. Six months. I joined the campaign in June.

STEPHEN. Six? Really?

MOLLY. Yup.

STEPHEN. Jesus. I must seem like a total asshole right now.

MOLLY. Not at all. *(Teasing.)* You're a big man on campus. I'm just a lowly intern.

STEPHEN. Come on. It's not like that.

MOLLY. Sure it is.

STEPHEN. No — it's just I meet so many people, have to remember so many names. I'm not always very good at remembering them all. But I remember faces. I always remember faces.

MOLLY. Like mine? *(Stephen stares at her, a bit taken aback, but not betraying it.)* Anyway …

STEPHEN. Why don't you sit down and have a drink with me.

MOLLY. Umm …

STEPHEN. One drink.

MOLLY. I should really get back to the office. I just ran out to give this envelope to you.

STEPHEN. I'll buy.

MOLLY. I don't know …

STEPHEN. Since you trekked all the way out here from the office.

MOLLY. It's only five blocks.

STEPHEN. In the snow.

MOLLY. Two inches.

STEPHEN. Without a jacket.

MOLLY. It wasn't very far.

STEPHEN. You're shivering.

MOLLY. No, I'm not. And I'm supposed to be back already.

STEPHEN. Fine. I won't be offended in the least that you turned down a drink with me.

MOLLY. No no no — I'd love to have a drink with you. I mean — yeah. I just really oughtta — … We're totally swamped, you know?

STEPHEN. Totally. So don't let me keep you.

MOLLY. Okay. But um … I'll probably be done with my stuff around ten if you … I don't know.

STEPHEN. If I what?

MOLLY. Well, I'll be done at ten or so, that's all.

STEPHEN.  Why don't you meet me here at eleven. I'll be done by then too.

MOLLY.  Here?

STEPHEN.  Right here. Right at this table. At eleven.

MOLLY.  Okay. At eleven. *(She exits. Stephen gulps down the rest of his drink. He pulls out the sheaf of papers from the packet and begins to look them over. Ben returns with a drink.)*

BEN.  That the stuff for the press conference tonight?

STEPHEN.  Yeah.

BEN.  Would it be helpful if I came? You know — to like pass stuff out or something.

STEPHEN.  No — I need you back at the office finishing up those press releases.

BEN.  I already finished them.

STEPHEN.  All of them?

BEN.  Yeah.

STEPHEN.  Then you should get started on next week's.

BEN.  I've already got drafts of those ready.

STEPHEN.  You shouldn't work yourself so hard, Ben. We've got eight more months of this.

BEN.  I just like staying on top of the work. So can I come to the press conference with you? It's just that I'm trying to learn everything I can and I thought — *(Stephen's cell begins to ring. Stephen puts down the papers and grabs his cell phone.)*

STEPHEN.  *(Not recognizing the number.)* Who the fuck is this?

BEN.  I thought you could use some help and —

STEPHEN.  *(Answering the phone.)* This is Steve. *(A perturbed look overtakes Stephen's face.)* How did you get this number? … Hold on a sec. *(Covering the phone. To Ben.)* Go get yourself another drink.

BEN.  *(Holding up his drink.)* But I —

STEPHEN.  Do it. *(Ben exits with his drink. Into the phone.)* I'm back … What for? … Not unless you tell me … Well, if it's that important shouldn't you be calling Paul? … Why? … I really shouldn't until I talk to Paul first … He's my boss. I can't just — … Look, this doesn't sound right to me … I've gotta be at a — … *(Stephen looks visibly torn as he listens.)* Yeah, I'm here … *(Grabs a pen from his jacket.)* Okay, where? … *(Cradles the phone and writes on a napkin.)* Uh-huh … Yeah, I know where that is … Alright, see you in a few. *(He hangs up. A moment passes as he considers what just occurred. He picks up his phone again and dials.)* Hello, Paul? …

Yeah, it's me. I just got a … *(He changes his mind.)* You know what — it's not important … Yeah, no. Just something stupid I really shouldn't be bothering you with. Have a great flight. I'll talk to you tomorrow … Okay. *(He hangs up. Another moment passes. He stands, yells to Ben.)* HEY, BEN — GO AHEAD AND MEET ME AT THE PRESS CONFERENCE. I MIGHT BE A FEW MINUTES LATE. *(He grabs the napkin and exits.)*

## Scene 2

*A rundown restaurant in East Des Moines. The furniture is shabby and the place is desolate except for Tom, who sits at a table alone, a briefcase beside him. Stephen enters. He approaches Tom's table.*

STEPHEN. Tom.

TOM. Steve. Thanks for coming. Please … take a load off.

STEPHEN. *(Sitting.)* I've got a press conference in about twenty minutes.

TOM. I know. You want a drink?

STEPHEN. No, thanks.

TOM. Let me buy you a drink.

STEPHEN. A Coke.

TOM. A *Coke?* Okay, a Coke. *(He signals a waiter.)* You look tired.

STEPHEN. I am.

TOM. Me too. This whole thing, it's turned into quite a ballbuster, huh?.

STEPHEN. Yeah.

TOM. Totally exhausting. Try to take care of myself though. That's one thing I've learned — gotta find the time to exercise, eat right. Hit the StairMaster every morning. Three squares a day. It's important when you get to be an old man like me. Young guy like you can live off adrenaline for six months straight and be just fine. I was that way when I was your age. *(A waiter approaches.)* We'll take a Sapphire and tonic … and a Coke.

WAITER. I'm sorry, we don't have Sapphire.

TOM.  Tanqueray?

WAITER.  No, I'm uh …

TOM.  Whatever you've got is fine.

WAITER.  Yes, sir. *(The waiter exits.)*

TOM.  'Course a little gin doesn't hurt. Gets the blood moving. Gotta drink something to keep warm. Cold as hell in this city, isn't it? And with this snow now …

STEPHEN.  What's this about, Tom?

TOM.  There's a lot of talk about you.

STEPHEN.  What sort of talk?

TOM.  You can stop looking around, Steve. There's no one here.

STEPHEN.  I wasn't, I was —

TOM.  Sure you were. I understand why you'd be worried. But give me a little credit. You think I'd pick a place where there was gonna be anybody?

STEPHEN.  Look, Tom, you said on the phone that this was important.

TOM.  Well — it's simple.

STEPHEN.  What is?

TOM.  You're working for the wrong man.

STEPHEN.  I'm sorry?

TOM.  You are working for the wrong man.

STEPHEN.  *(Laughs.)* That's funny.

TOM.  You're a smart guy, Steve. Very smart. But there's a lot of smart guys out there. Eventually they make a wrong move or get too arrogant or get too paranoid or just plain buckle under all the pressure. You know what I'm talking about. The heels at your back. Guys twice your age jealous of you. Younger guys circling like vultures. You start making enemies you don't even know you had. That's a terrible feeling, isn't it? Constantly looking over your shoulder, wondering who you can trust. Always wondering / who is going to screw you next.

STEPHEN.  Okay — look — I appreciate the advice, but I really don't —

TOM.  You've got something the other guys don't have. You've got a special — … what is it? Charm isn't the right word. It's more than that. You *exude* something. You draw people in. All the reporters love you. Even the ones that hate you love you. We both know how much work it takes, constantly being on guard, weighing every word so carefully, every move. But you make it look easy. People are scared of you because they don't understand how you do it, and they love you for it. There's nothing more valuable in this business — the ability to win people's respect by making them mistake their fear for love.

STEPHEN.  If you're trying to poach me — you're wasting your time.

TOM.  You are going to *lose* Iowa.

STEPHEN.  Bullshit. *(Tom takes a folder out of his briefcase and slips it across the table to Stephen.)*

TOM.  Look inside. *(Stephen opens the folder. There are a few pieces of paper inside. Stephen glances at them.)*

STEPHEN.  This can't be real.

TOM.  It's very real.

STEPHEN.  So you're telling me every other poll on the planet is off?

TOM.  Exactly.

STEPHEN.  That's impossible.

TOM.  Twenty percent of what you think is your solid support is actually our people posing as Morris supporters. Inflates your lead, makes you feel comfortable, makes us look like the underdog. Three days ago we started telling them to switch back over to us when the pollsters call. During the next week the tracks will show us gaining steadily and finally overtaking you a day before the caucus. It'll look like we've made a come-from-behind victory, when in reality we've had the lead all along. We'll have the momentum out of Iowa and take New Hampshire on the twenty-seventh. Morris will throw in the towel by Super Tuesday.

STEPHEN.  There's no way you could have organized that many people and kept it a secret.

TOM.  Our field director talks to fifty organizers. Each of those organizers talk to a dozen precinct captains. The precinct captains call twenty, thirty supporters they trust. Do the math, Steve. That's what — fifteen thousand voters. Over ten percent of the vote.

STEPHEN.  You're lying.

TOM.  What good would it do me to show you these numbers if they weren't real?

STEPHEN.  And you're dumb enough to show them to me?

TOM.  Take them. Have Morris hit every county in the state. You might pick up a point or two, but you don't have enough time to close the gap. I'm not showing you these numbers to try and intimidate you, Steve. I'm showing you these numbers because I want you to work for a winner.

STEPHEN. I *am* working for a winner.

TOM. Wrong. These numbers are just the tip of the iceberg. A week ago I brought three hundred more field staff to pump up the GOTV. The day before the caucus we'll robocall and mass mail the hell out of your supporters with wrong polling locations. On game day I'll send vans out to your strong areas to cause traffic jams so your supporters can't get to their caucuses. And once everyone gets into the caucus room you'll find that a third of your precinct captains are actually our people. And by the way — we've got Thompson in the bag.

STEPHEN. I know for a fact that Thompson is going with us.

TOM. We promised Thompson Secretary of Labor, so he'll do anything we tell him to do — like sticking a carrot in front of your noses until we tell him to yank it away. Iowa's already over, Steve. It's been over for weeks. I'm thinking way down the road now. That's why I want you. We need the best. I'll bring you in straight at the top. *(Stephen closes the folder and slides it back across the table.)*

STEPHEN. I've played dirty before. Done stuff that keeps me awake at night. But this …

TOM. It'll win us the nomination.

STEPHEN. It's illegal.

TOM. Of course it is.

STEPHEN. This is the sort of shit the Republicans pull.

TOM. You're right, this is exactly what the Republicans do, and it's about time we learned from them. They're meaner, tougher and more disciplined than we are. I've been in this business for thirty years, and I've seen way too many Democrats bite the dust because they wouldn't get down in the mud with the elephants.

STEPHEN. If I took this to the press you'd be fucked.

TOM. Try it. There's no way to prove anything. Not a single paper trail, not a single email, nothing. It would take reporters months to get something solid, and by that time we've already won the nomination. Then you'd just be screwing over the Democratic Party, and I know you don't want that.

STEPHEN. I could never work for someone like you.

TOM. People like me get keys to the White House. You want your set of keys, you better learn to work for people like me.

STEPHEN. How would it look if I jumped ship a week before the caucus and joined you guys? I'd be branded as the most disloyal, opportunistic asshole ever. My credibility would be totally shot.

And the media would go ape-shit.

TOM. You had irreconcilable differences with senior staff, that's all you need to say.

STEPHEN. But that's not true.

TOM. It doesn't have to be.

STEPHEN. No — Look. I shouldn't even be sitting here right now. I shouldn't even be having this conversation. *(The waiter approaches with the drinks. Sets them down.)*

WAITER. One gin and tonic. One Coke. Are you ready to order?

STEPHEN. I'm leaving.

TOM. *(To the waiter.)* My friend's gotta be somewhere to be in a few minutes, what can you bring out quickly?

WAITER. The uh, the buffalo wings would probably be the fastest.

STEPHEN. I told you, I'm leaving.

TOM. Two minutes, Steve.

STEPHEN. I don't —

TOM. *(To the waiter.)* An order of buffalo wings. *(The waiter exits. To Stephen.)* Stay. Two more minutes.

STEPHEN. The answer is no.

TOM. The answer is maybe. If the answer was no — you wouldn't have shown up in the first place. I know you want this. Otherwise you would've told me to go fuck myself by now.

STEPHEN. Then go fuck yourself. *(Stephen stands.)*

TOM. Don't flush your career down the drain. You don't give me two minutes and I will shut you out once we win the nomination. You will work for no one. You don't have to tell me straightaway. Sleep on it, think it over. But I need to know soon. I want you before the caucus, not after you've lost. At that point it just looks like you're jumping on the bandwagon.

STEPHEN. I couldn't do this to Paul.

TOM. Fuck Paul. Paul's only ever worked for insurgent wackos that never had a chance of winning, just like he is now. I'm giving you a chance to leap right over Paul and be bigger than he ever was.

STEPHEN. Paul's a friend.

TOM. The question you gotta ask yourself is whether you want friends, or whether you want to work for the President.

STEPHEN. I won't do it.

TOM. Thanks for the two minutes. You have my number. *(Stephen exits.)*

# Scene 3

*Early the next morning. A room in the Hotel Fort Des Moines. Clothes are scattered about the room. Stephen stands in his underwear, talking into a cell phone. As he talks, Molly enters from the bathroom and begins to get dressed.*

STEPHEN. Hey, Paul — it's me — trying you again. *(Looks at his watch.)* You're probably on the plane by now, but I just wanted to see how things went with Thompson. If you get this before you take off, gimme a call. *(He ends the call, immediately speed dials another.)* Hey, Ben? It's Steve … What time does Paul's plane get in this morning? … Okay, I need you to find out — the airline, the flight number — … Right … *(Looks at his phone, sees another call is coming in, back into the phone.)* Hey look, Ida's calling on the other line, get back to me with that info, okay? *(He switches over to the other line.)* What's up, Ida? … Uh-huh … I guess we'll have to see how good the roads are … *(Laughs.)* Maybe we can have him build a fucking snowman or shovel the driveway at an orphanage … *(Laughs.)* Come on, Ida, you know and I know that's a load of bull-shit, and so does everyone else, so don't try to bait me — not this early in the morning … *(Laughs.)*
MOLLY. *(Whispers to him.)* Do you want me to go?
STEPHEN. *(Covers the phone.)* Stick around for a minute. *(Back into the phone.)* Hey — did you get the press release on the — … Sure it's a story … You said you'd keep an open mind if I was trying to push anything, so here I am pushing it. We're gonna play nice with each other, right? — … Well look, why don't we meet in the lobby. I'll be downstairs in a half-hour tops … Okay, good. See you then. *(He hangs up.)*
MOLLY. You seem busy. I don't wanna intrude or anything.
STEPHEN. No — we should talk about — *(Stephen's phone rings.)* This is Steve … Uh-huh … No no no, you gotta look at the report too, Frank, that's where the real good stuff is … Name me one renewable energy bill that Pullman got to the floor which was halfway meaningful … That one doesn't count … The numbers,

Frank, that's all I'm saying. Look at the numbers and then look at his record — there's your story …

MOLLY. Hey Steve?

STEPHEN. *(Into the phone.)* You guys have been begging for more issue shit, so now I'm giving it to you and —

MOLLY. Steve?

STEPHEN. *(Covering the phone.)* What's up?

MOLLY. I'm gonna go.

STEPHEN. *(Into the phone, holding up a finger for Molly to wait.)* Yeah, but you're missing the point … *(Molly heads for the door anyway, starts to open it. Into the phone:)* Hold on a sec, Frank *(Covering the phone.)* Don't go yet.

MOLLY. You have work to do.

STEPHEN. Wait a minute. I wanna talk to you about something. *(During the following Molly picks up one of the newspapers on the bed and peruses it. Into the phone.)* Frank? Sorry about that … Nobody, just the uh, the cleaning lady. What was I saying? Oh right, I was saying you're missing the fucking point. What this is about is — … *(Glances over at Molly.)* Hey, Frank? Look, I got a meeting with Paul I really got to run to. Can I call you later about this? Yeah, that's good … Okay, talk to you soon. *(He hangs up. Referring to the phone.)* Alright, I'm putting this down.

MOLLY. The cleaning lady?

STEPHEN. What?

MOLLY. You told him I was the cleaning lady.

STEPHEN. Oh, that — come on. I / was just —

MOLLY. It's fine. I don't care.

STEPHEN. Look — it was just easier to —

MOLLY. Really — I don't care.

STEPHEN. Okay, I just don't want you / to think —

MOLLY. You said you wanted to talk to me about something?

STEPHEN. Yeah — I just wanna … how do I put this? I just want to be clear about everything so there's no confusion, to make sure we understand each other.

MOLLY. I won't tell anyone about last night.

STEPHEN. No no, it's not that. I mean, yes, I'd appreciate if we kept this … if you could be discreet, because, I mean, you know how people are …

MOLLY. Wouldn't look good that you screwed an intern.

STEPHEN. Hey now …

MOLLY.  Yes. I know how people are.

STEPHEN.  They look for every opportunity to —

MOLLY.  I get it. Don't worry. Your secret is safe.

STEPHEN.  Okay.

MOLLY.  So.

STEPHEN.  So what I wanted to talk to you about was that …
alright, the truth is I have — I *had* — I don't know, it's complicated. I *had* this girlfriend back in D.C., a pretty serious girlfriend.
And things have been rocky lately so we're kind of taking a break,
but I'm not really looking to get into anything serious, you know?
Or even want to give the hint of that, so —

MOLLY.  You told me all of this last night.

STEPHEN.  What?

MOLLY.  Your girlfriend. How you guys have been having trouble …

STEPHEN.  I told you about that?

MOLLY.  Her name is Helen, right?

STEPHEN.  Yeah.

MOLLY.  You told me all about her.

STEPHEN.  When did I …

MOLLY.  At the bar. You don't remember? You kept telling me how
much you love her. How much you miss her.

STEPHEN.  I did?

MOLLY.  You talked on and on about her.

STEPHEN.  I must have been really fucking drunk.

MOLLY.  I think we were both pretty drunk.

STEPHEN.  Wait — last night — did I say anything about — …
*(Stopping himself.)*

MOLLY.  About what?

STEPHEN.  Besides what I said about, Helen. Did I — … I just
talked about Helen right?

MOLLY.  Pretty much.

STEPHEN.  Not about anything else?

MOLLY.  What are you getting at?

STEPHEN.  You know what? Never mind. It's not important.
*(Changing the subject, laughs to himself.)* Man, you must think I'm
a complete dipshit …

MOLLY.  No — I don't.

STEPHEN.  'Cause it's not like I just got totally wasted and this
thing happened because … I mean, I wanted to. I really like you.
You're smart as fuck. You're gorgeous … but I just … well, I wanted

to talk to you because I don't want there to be any expectations, because I —

MOLLY. Stephen — you don't have to say anything.

STEPHEN. I just don't want you to think that I'm some sort of player.

MOLLY. Well, you *are* kind of a player, but that's okay.

STEPHEN. No, I'm not.

MOLLY. The way you asked me to sit down and have a drink with you.

STEPHEN. I was just being polite.

MOLLY. Bullshit.

STEPHEN. I *was.*

MOLLY. You were hitting on me.

STEPHEN. No, I wasn't.

MOLLY. It was totally obvious.

STEPHEN. I was *obvious?*

MOLLY. *So* obvious.

STEPHEN. I thought I was being all smooth and subtle.

MOLLY. You were pretty forward about it.

STEPHEN. You were pretty forward yourself, telling me when you got off work.

MOLLY. Well, yeah. I've been wanting to get in your pants for a long time.

STEPHEN. Really?

MOLLY. Back in headquarters, when you'd stroll into the office … yeah. I couldn't keep my eyes off you.

STEPHEN. I never knew.

MOLLY. Because you didn't know I existed.

STEPHEN. So when you came with the envelope …

MOLLY. It wasn't supposed to be me that was gonna bring it. Jerry was gonna bring it over, but I told him I'd do it 'cause I wanted to see you.

STEPHEN. So you totally planned on …

MOLLY. Yup.

STEPHEN. Wearing those ass-hugging jeans and that shirt …

MOLLY. I changed before I came to the hotel.

STEPHEN. I played right into your hands.

MOLLY. Exactly.

STEPHEN. Wow.

MOLLY. Pretty slutty of me, huh?

STEPHEN. No — not at all. I mean — I kind of respect it — in a weird sort of way — how you — yeah.

MOLLY. Good.

STEPHEN. So you're cool with this, you know, with where I'm at and —

MOLLY. We had fun. That's all it was.

STEPHEN. We *did* have fun, didn't we?

MOLLY. If you remember it.

STEPHEN. Of course I remember.

MOLLY. Well you seemed to have blacked out about the —

STEPHEN. I remember coming back here okay. That I completely remember.

MOLLY. You passed out right after we had sex.

STEPHEN. No, I didn't.

MOLLY. You said, "I gotta get up really early baby. Guh-night." Then you rolled over and passed out.

STEPHEN. I *did* have to get up early.

MOLLY. It was cute. I watched you sleep for a little while. You snored.

STEPHEN. Oh shit. Was it loud?

MOLLY. No, it was kind of adorable actually. Like a kitten. You didn't really snore. You purred.

STEPHEN. I *purred?*

MOLLY. It was like. *(Molly purrs. Stephen laughs.)* Are you gonna tell her about me?

STEPHEN. Who?

MOLLY. Your girlfriend.

STEPHEN. Um ... I don't know. Like I said — it's complicated.

MOLLY. You said last night that you usually tell her when you hook up with someone.

STEPHEN. That's the deal we have. If one of us — you know — we tell each other.

MOLLY. Even though you're broken up?

STEPHEN. Do we have to talk about this?

MOLLY. Sorry, I —

STEPHEN. It's fine.

MOLLY. You can tell her, though. I know it's none of my business, and I know I don't have to give you permission, but in case you're wondering — I don't mind if you tell her.

STEPHEN. You're incredibly mature.

MOLLY. For a teenager.

STEPHEN. That's not what I meant.

MOLLY. It *is* what you meant.

STEPHEN. Come on.

MOLLY. Did it turn you on?

STEPHEN. What?

MOLLY. That I'm so young.

STEPHEN. No. I mean — you're hot. You're smart —

MOLLY. It did — didn't it?

STEPHEN. Well, sure. Not in some like, pedophile way, but yeah.

MOLLY. When's the last time you bagged a nineteen-year-old?

STEPHEN. Uh … shit. I don't know. Awhile I guess. Now you're really making me feel like an old man.

MOLLY. You *are* an old man.

STEPHEN. Twenty-five isn't old.

MOLLY. You were in college when I got my first period.

STEPHEN. Very funny.

MOLLY. When I was born you could already do basic arithmetic.

STEPHEN. Did it turn *you* on? That I'm older?

MOLLY. Maybe.

STEPHEN. Landing the older man?

MOLLY. Well, you're not the first.

STEPHEN. What do you mean?

MOLLY. I've been with a lot of older guys.

STEPHEN. Really?

MOLLY. You're like the youngest I've ever been with.

STEPHEN. Bullshit.

MOLLY. It's true. I've never dated a guy younger than twenty-five.

STEPHEN. Even in high school?

MOLLY. I had an affair with my English teacher when I was fifteen. During a year abroad in France.

STEPHEN. Holy shit.

MOLLY. He was harmless. I'm the one who seduced him. I mean, it was pretty obvious he wanted me. I'd go over to his house to help him grade papers all the time. Even used to babysit his kids.

STEPHEN. And the others?

MOLLY. What others?

STEPHEN. You said you'd been with *lots* of older guys.

MOLLY. Well, I guess not *lots,* but a few.

STEPHEN. Tell me, tell me. *(At some point during the following she*

34

*starts flipping through one of the newspapers on the bed.)*
MOLLY.  All right — *so* … I took a year off between high school and college and moved in with this guy Peter. He was twenty-nine — a chef at this restaurant where I waited tables. He got really needy and possessive. Asked me to marry him as soon as I turned eighteen. Freaked me out. I said, "Maybe when I graduate from college," but as soon as I got to school I never spoke to him again. And then my first semester I dated a drummer in this band. Luke. He was thirty-one. I ended it after a few months because when it came down to it, he really wasn't the sharpest knife in the rack. And when I left school to join the campaign — well, there's been a couple people on the campaign. Where's that renewable energy story? I don't see it anywhere.
STEPHEN.  Who?
MOLLY.  What?
STEPHEN.  Who else on the campaign?
MOLLY.  Just hook-ups, nothing serious.
STEPHEN.  Like who?
MOLLY.  I don't know … Matt Spenser, on and off for a few weeks.
STEPHEN.  That douche bag?
MOLLY.  He's hot.
STEPHEN.  Who else?
MOLLY.  Nobody.
STEPHEN.  You said a couple.
MOLLY.  You're prying.
STEPHEN.  Tell me.
MOLLY.  Why should I?
STEPHEN.  I spilled my guts about my girlfriend.
MOLLY.  When you were wasted.
STEPHEN.  You afraid I'm gonna tell somebody?
MOLLY.  No …
STEPHEN.  So what's the harm? *(Molly considers this for a moment.)*
MOLLY.  You promise you won't tell a soul?
STEPHEN.  Scout's honor.
MOLLY.  I'm not joking.
STEPHEN.  Yes. I won't tell anyone.
MOLLY.  Well, once, a couple months ago, I … — Wow. I can't believe I'm telling you this.
STEPHEN.  Come on, come on, come on.

MOLLY. Paul …

STEPHEN. Paul who?

MOLLY. *Paul.*

STEPHEN. Paul Zara?

MOLLY. Just once.

STEPHEN. No way.

MOLLY. Yeah.

STEPHEN. Paul fucking *Zara?*

MOLLY. You see — I shouldn't have told you.

STEPHEN. No, no. I'm just surprised.

MOLLY. You can't tell anyone.

STEPHEN. I won't. No … I'm just — … Wow. How did it happen?

MOLLY. What — you want me to break it down for you…?

STEPHEN. Yeah, break it down for me.

MOLLY. It's really not that interesting.

STEPHEN. This was back at headquarters?

MOLLY. I really don't want to talk about it.

STEPHEN. Did he proposition you or something?

MOLLY. Steve …

STEPHEN. Okay, okay. It's just totally — man. You fucked my boss. Kind of working your way down the line, huh?

MOLLY. That's a nasty thing to say.

STEPHEN. I didn't mean it like that.

MOLLY. How *did* you mean it?

STEPHEN. I was joking.

MOLLY. Well, it wasn't funny.

STEPHEN. I'm sorry.

MOLLY. You're the only person I've ever told.

STEPHEN. That's a good thing. You definitely don't want that to get around.

MOLLY. I don't even know why I said anything. I promised Paul I / wouldn't ever …

STEPHEN. Look — you can tell me anything, okay? Really. I know how to keep a secret.

MOLLY. I know, I know.

STEPHEN. Molly — I think you are — you're an amazing woman. Incredible, actually. It's like — *(Stephen's phone rings.)*

MOLLY. You should take that.

STEPHEN. This is Steve … Yeah … Uh-huh … Hey, Chris, we're all gonna get together and go over that before the background

36

briefing. I'm right in the middle of something, so let me call you back, okay? … Alright, bye. *(He hangs up.)*

MOLLY.  I should go.

STEPHEN.  Stay. Let's mess up these sheets a little more.

MOLLY.  You have to meet with Ida.

STEPHEN.  Not for another fifteen minutes.

MOLLY.  But I need to get to the office.

STEPHEN.  Well, I'm not gonna beg you to stay.

MOLLY.  Begging doesn't suit you.

STEPHEN.  *(Chuckles.)* You know, twenty-four hours ago I was just minding my business, doing my job, getting ready for a press conference. And in you waltz with your little envelope and your ass-hugging jeans … And now? Here I am —

MOLLY.  With a nineteen-year-old intern lying in your bed.

STEPHEN.  With a nineteen-year-old intern lying in my bed. *(Molly stands.)*

MOLLY.  Seriously, though — we both have work to do.

STEPHEN.  There's nothing I can do to convince you to stay.

MOLLY.  You're starting to beg.

STEPHEN.  Call me later?

MOLLY.  *(She gives him a kiss.)* You call me. If you can remember … *(She leaves. Stephen paces for a moment. Now that Molly is gone, reality is setting in. He grabs his cell phone off the table and dials.)*

STEPHEN.  Hey, Ben — it's me again. I'm still waiting on that fuckin' info about Paul's flight. Get it to me pronto, okay? … Good … And another thing — send an email out to the press corps telling them we're gonna reschedule the background briefing for later this afternoon … Alright, talk to you in a few. *(He hangs up.)*

## Scene 4

*The main terminal at the Des Moines airport. Stephen is waiting nervously. Paul approaches him from behind, pulling his roll-away suitcase.*

PAUL. Boo! *(Stephen whips around, startled.)*
STEPHEN. Paul.
PAUL. What're you doin' here?
STEPHEN. Thought I'd pick you up myself.
PAUL. *(Teasing him.)* That was sweet of you. I'm touched. Truly.
STEPHEN. Good flight? *(Paul sets his suitcase aside, pulls a tin of chewing tobacco out of his back pocket and wedges some chew in his cheek.)*
PAUL. Been *dying* the last three hours. Rude to spit into a cup when someone's sittin' next to you. I need to find another addiction is what I need to do. This snow — we circled so many times I thought they were gonna re-route us to fuckin' Omaha. How long you been waiting?
STEPHEN. 'Bout an hour.
PAUL. Sorry you had to wait.
STEPHEN. Don't worry about it.
PAUL. Seriously, it was nice of you to come out here and pick me up. I coulda gotten a cab you know.
STEPHEN. Well, I got a rental this morning, so …
PAUL. I hope not an expensive one.
STEPHEN. On my own dime.
PAUL. You shouldn't've done that. If you needed a car, we could've —
STEPHEN. We need to talk.
PAUL. You're sounding way too serious.
STEPHEN. Did you get my messages?
PAUL. No — I haven't turned my phone on yet.
STEPHEN. What'd Thompson say?
PAUL. Cocksucker said he's having second thoughts.
STEPHEN. Shit.
PAUL. I know. Thought this trip was to seal it, but I get to his

house this morning and he starts throwin' up smoke right and left, says he wants to see how things pan out in Iowa. I almost rip him a new asshole, but I stop myself. I ask him — why'd you have me fly all the way out here just to tell me you're not sure? He says he needs more info — what our strategy is over the next ten days, all this shit.

STEPHEN. Did you tell him?

PAUL. 'Course I told him. Talked his ear off for an hour — exactly how we're gonna take Iowa, every single step. And *still* no dice.

STEPHEN. This is bad Paul.

PAUL. What is?

STEPHEN. Thompson's not gonna endorse.

PAUL. He's just playin' a little hard to get.

STEPHEN. No, Paul — he's definitely not gonna endorse.

PAUL. What are you talking about?

STEPHEN. He's gonna endorse Pullman three days out. Fuck — I should have called you last night, but I was hoping it wasn't true. I should have —

PAUL. Whoa whoa whoa — slow down.

STEPHEN. Look Paul — I met with Tom Duffy last night.

PAUL. You *what?*

STEPHEN. He called me just after you left for the airport and asked to meet. I asked what it was about, and he said it was really important. So I did. I met with him. Shit, I should've called / you. I —

PAUL. Stop. Let me get this straight. You met with Tom Duffy?

STEPHEN. Yes.

PAUL. What'd he want?

STEPHEN. Well first he — look — the gist of it is he wants to hire me. He wants me to jump ship and come work for him. This is bad, Paul. He showed me poll numbers with Pullman already ahead by four. They've been telling their supporters to pose as Morris people to the pollsters. We're in really deep fucking trouble.

PAUL. That can't be true. He was playing mind games with you.

STEPHEN. He laid out their whole plan. Robocalls, traffic jams, fake lit and fucking Thompson. Promised him Secretary of Labor and told him to lead us on. Everything you told him today's gonna go straight to Duffy's ear.

PAUL. If this is some sort of practical — I mean — my blood pressure is going through the roof right now.

STEPHEN. I'm sorry, Paul. I really should have called / you.

PAUL.  This happened last night?

STEPHEN.  Just before the press conference.

PAUL.  And you didn't *call* me?

STEPHEN.  I'm sorry, Paul. I — I don't know. I guess I thought — I thought maybe it wasn't true. Maybe / he was —

PAUL.  Jesus, Steve. I can't believe you didn't —

STEPHEN.  I know I know I know. Look — I was scared. I was scared and totally confused, and I thought —

PAUL.  It doesn't *matter* what you thought. It matters what you did. It matters what you *didn't* do. If all this shit is true I made an ass of myself at Thompson's place. And I gave away our whole goddamn strategy. Just handed it over.

STEPHEN.  I know, Paul. Believe me. But it's like — like I was paralyzed. I didn't know if it was even worth telling you about if — if you came back and said — yeah — Thompson's in the bag, but … fuck, Paul. I don't know.

PAUL.  I sure as hell hope you were gonna tell me even if I came back and —

STEPHEN.  Of course! Yes. I just —

PAUL.  'Cause I mean, if you were planning on keeping this secret —

STEPHEN.  No! Not at all. That's why I'm telling you now.

PAUL.  After I tell you Thompson said no.

STEPHEN.  Seriously, Paul, that's why I'm here now. To tell you. To —

PAUL.  A little late now, don't you think? After I —

STEPHEN.  You know me, Paul. You know I would never — I really should have called last night. I should have and I didn't.

PAUL.  You're fucking right you should have. You don't meet secretly with the other guy's campaign manager and *not* fucking tell me about it. You don't get a fucking *phone call* from the other guy's manager and not tell me.

STEPHEN.  This is the *first* time Paul. The first time I've ever really fucked up. And I'm sorry. I am so sorry.

PAUL.  It's a pretty big goddamn fuck-up whether it's your first time or not. I mean if we lose here, if we *lose* — it's over, we're dead.

STEPHEN.  We can figure this out. There has to be a way to figure this out.

PAUL.  We *better* figure this the fuck out.

STEPHEN.  Paul. Please. You gotta forgive me on this. I feel like absolute shit. I feel terrible. Last night, I was so — you want to

40

know the truth? I was so wound up about this shit that I went out and got wasted. Totally wasted. Drank myself to oblivion. Slept with some girl I shouldn't have. I dealt with this completely the wrong way. So I'm coming clean now. I came out to the airport to tell you this so we can figure it out. I know if we put our heads together and we — Goddamnit! I'm sorry. I am so so so —

PAUL. Steve.

STEPHEN. I am *so* sorry. I feel like I'm — I feel like —

PAUL. Steve. Stop. It's okay.

STEPHEN. No it isn't.

PAUL. It is. It's okay. You're right. We can figure it out. You did the right thing. You told me, which means that we can do something about it.

STEPHEN. I know there's a way.

PAUL. There's always a way. So take a breath and get yourself together. I need you at your best on this.

STEPHEN. I don't want you to think — I mean — I respect the hell out of you, and your respect is something I —

PAUL. You and I are still okay, alright? It's been me and you from the beginning on this thing, and I got a little upset, but that's just because all of this — it's a bit of a shock to me. You're allowed your one fuck-up. So now let's get past that and get to work. Sound good?

STEPHEN. Yeah.

PAUL. Good. Now. First thing we have to do is get to that fucking event in — where is it?

STEPHEN. Cedar Rapids.

PAUL. Cedar Rapids. We got to get to that event in Cedar Rapids so I can break this all to the Governor. You can fill me in on the drive out there — everthing that happened with Duffy — every detail.

STEPHEN. The Governor's gonna flip.

PAUL. He'll be fine. I know how to handle him. You just do your job and deal with the press.

STEPHEN. I can do that.

PAUL. Of course you can.

STEPHEN. Thanks, Paul. Really.

PAUL. Don't thank me. Just win me this fuckin' state.

## End of Act One

41

# ACT TWO

## Scene 1

*An event in Cedar Rapids later that day. Stephen is standing outside an elementary school gym talking with Frank, a reporter from the* Los Angeles Times. *Ben is waiting just off to the side. Occasionally we hear the muffled cheers of the event inside the gym.*

STEPHEN.  Of course they're tightening. That's what happens a week out.

FRANK.  And you're not worried?

STEPHEN.  No. We've held the lead for three months. Our base is strong. Ninety-five percent of the people who are going to vote have already made their choice. You're just seeing a few undecided going the other way.

FRANK.  But your numbers are sliding. This isn't just a few undecideds suddenly —

STEPHEN.  Three points? That's hardly a slide, Frank. Like I said, we're a week out. You've covered these things before. The race tightens. That's how it goes.

FRANK.  It keeps going like this, you'll be within the margin of error by Friday.

STEPHEN.  So let it. We started out as the underdog and proved everyone wrong, we'll do it again. You know and I know that half of this shit is the press. You all want a tight race, so you've been slamming us, and now you're getting your tight race.

FRANK.  You can't blame this on us.

STEPHEN.  I sure as hell can. When's the last time you wrote an article that had anything to do with one of our events?

FRANK.  I write about your events.

STEPHEN.  A line. Maybe two, on a good day. Then you regurgitate Pullman's oppo for the next three columns.

FRANK. You're not being fair.

STEPHEN. Don't talk to me about fair, Frank. None of this shit is fair. If you all were being fair, I'd wake up to a much different stack of papers every morning.

FRANK. What's gotten into you, Stevie?

STEPHEN. Nothing's gotten into me.

FRANK. I ask you a few questions — you blow up at me.

STEPHEN. You're missing the event, Frank.

FRANK. Is something going on?

STEPHEN. The event — right through those doors.

FRANK. Off the record.

STEPHEN. Nothing. Really. Now please, go watch this event. I'd still like our line or two in tomorrow's paper.

FRANK. There's only so many ways I can cover a stump speech, Stevie. It's the same speech every time. *(A massive cheer of the crowd is heard within.)*

STEPHEN. You hear that? It's the same speech because it works. This guy is gonna be the next president of the United States, and you're standing out here talking to me. Go in there and do your job. You oughtta be listening to him instead of hounding my ass about the tracking polls. Don't you think the people of Los Angeles deserve to get a little accurate reportage? Or do they even read the paper?

FRANK. *(He's had enough.)* You want me to soften up on you guys — bitching me out isn't exactly the best way to go about it.

STEPHEN. Well, I'm tired of sucking your cock.

FRANK. Jesus, Steve — you need to get some sleep. *(Frank exits into the event. Ben approaches Stephen.)*

BEN. Steve.

STEPHEN. Why the fuck are you always lurking around? *(Beat.)* Don't you have press releases to hand out?

BEN. I already did.

STEPHEN. Well, go hand out some more. *(Ben holds up a few sheets of paper.)*

BEN. I was wondering if you'd take a look at this.

STEPHEN. Can it wait?

BEN. I — well, I just —

STEPHEN. Yes or no? We're right in the middle of an event.

BEN. It's a speech.

STEPHEN. What speech?

BEN. For the governor. A new stump speech.

STEPHEN. I didn't put out an order for a new speech.

BEN. I know. I just figured ...

STEPHEN. Figured what?

BEN. I just figured that since the reporters were getting a little ... you know ... a little bored with — *(Stephen grabs the speech and looks it over.)*

STEPHEN. Who wrote this?

BEN. I did.

STEPHEN. You don't change a stump speech a week before the caucus.

BEN. Well, it's more than a stump speech — it's kind of a new approach. A whole new —

STEPHEN. We spent months — *I* spent months perfecting the Governor's speech. Every word. Every gesture. Every pause. You don't up and change your message seven days out.

BEN. I wasn't trying to imply that the Governor's speech isn't good, it's just a matter of how effective it is at this point, since all the reporters —

STEPHEN. Effective? It's put us in the lead for three months straight. *(Ida enters, coming from the event, and approaches Stephen as Ben talks.)*

BEN. Look, Steve — I was just hoping you'd look it over and tell me what you think, even if you don't want to use it.

STEPHEN. I don't.

BEN. You haven't read it, though.

STEPHEN. I just did.

BEN. You skimmed the first page.

STEPHEN. Did you hear a word I said? We're not gonna change the —

BEN. Well, maybe you could at least show it to Paul. I really think there's some good stuff in there, and if we just insert a few things into his regular —

STEPHEN. Another time, Ben. *(Stephen hands the speech back to Ben.)* What's up, Ida?

IDA. If you two are —

STEPHEN. No — not at all. Talk to me.

BEN. Can I just slip this under your door at the hotel and —

STEPHEN. Go away, Ben.

BEN. It'll be there when you get back.

STEPHEN. I said, go the fuck away. *(Ben leers at him for a second*

44

*— his frustration and anger seething — but he keeps his cool. His next line is delivered with confidence and dignity.)*

BEN.  Alright. We'll talk later then. When you're a little less busy. *(Ben exits.)*

IDA.  Wow. Kinda harsh there.

STEPHEN.  Kid wrote a — ... never mind. It's not important.

IDA.  I like, Ben. He's a sweetheart.

STEPHEN.  He's an ambitious little fucker.

IDA.  Look in a mirror darlin'.

STEPHEN.  Hangs around me like a puppy.

IDA.  He looks up to you. You're his idol.

STEPHEN.  *(Laughs bitterly.)* Whatever.

IDA.  So, Stevie ... off the record ...

STEPHEN.  No, Ida. I can't tell you what happened in South Carolina.

IDA.  That's not what I wanted to ask you about.

STEPHEN.  No?

IDA.  Well, not right away. There's something else.

STEPHEN.  I'm listening.

IDA.  You met with Tom Duffy. *(A pause. Stephen doesn't know what to say.)* So it's true?

STEPHEN.  Who told you that?

IDA.  A little bird.

STEPHEN.  Who?

IDA.  Did you meet with him?

STEPHEN.  Tell me who, Ida.

IDA.  Can't do that.

STEPHEN.  I'm not fucking around here.

IDA.  Neither am I.

STEPHEN.  It's not true.

IDA.  I *know* you met with him. At a little restaurant in East Des Moines, last night, just before the press conference. Duffy ordered buffalo wings.

STEPHEN.  Did Duffy tell you this?

IDA.  Anonymous.

STEPHEN.  You don't have shit.

IDA.  This is a story, Steve.

STEPHEN.  The *Times* won't print anything with one uncorroborated anonymous source.

IDA.  I can't get it printed at the *Times,* but I could always give

45

Matt Drudge a call …

STEPHEN. You're gonna play gutter ball with me?

IDA. All I'm saying is that you've got a choice. You tell me what happened with Duffy and I bury it, *or* the story shows up in a blurb somewhere. I just wanna be in the loop.

STEPHEN. I'm not gonna let you strong-arm me.

IDA. What happened with Duffy?

STEPHEN. You're supposed to be my friend, Ida. You'd stab me in the back like this? You'd ruin my reputation / just so you —

IDA. Wait wait wait — is that what you thought? That we were friends?

STEPHEN. I've given you *everything* — every fucking scoop, your profile with Paul …

IDA. You're right — you've given me a lot. But let's get real here, Steve. The only reason you ever treated me well was because I work for the *Times*. Not because I was your *friend*. You give me what I want, I write you better stories. Don't pretend it's any more than that.

STEPHEN. So this is the shit you're willing to pull to get your story?

IDA. You'd do the same if you were me.

STEPHEN. No, I wouldn't.

IDA. Go fuck yourself.

STEPHEN. Ask me a million times, I'm still not gonna —

IDA. Okay, I'll make it easier on you. Forget Duffy. What happened at Paul and Thompson's meeting?

STEPHEN. No.

IDA. Is he gonna endorse?

STEPHEN. You're not getting a goddamn thing out of me.

IDA. Don't make things hard on yourself.

STEPHEN. This conversation's over. *(Stephen starts walking away.)*

IDA. Do you really want this story getting out?

STEPHEN. *(Stopping.)* Lower your voice.

IDA. Do you?

STEPHEN. *(Coming back.)* Do you realize what a story like this could do to me?

IDA. Of course I do. That's why I'm giving you a choice here.

STEPHEN. I could get fired.

IDA. So it's not a difficult choice, is it? *(A pause as Stephen takes this in.)* I've got to file by four. You've got till then to make up your mind. *(Ida exits. Stephen pulls out his cell phone and dials. On the opposite side of the stage, lights come up on Tom sitting at a desk, his phone ringing. Tom looks at the number on his phone and answers.)*

TOM. Steve.

STEPHEN. You fuckin' bastard.

TOM. Excuse me?

STEPHEN. You leaked it.

TOM. Leaked what?

STEPHEN. Don't bullshit me, Tom.

TOM. Bullshit you? What the —

STEPHEN. I just spoke with Ida Horowicz.

TOM. Yeah?

STEPHEN. Why'd you do it?

TOM. Do what? What the hell are you talking about?

STEPHEN. You know exactly what I'm talking about.

TOM. No, Steve. I wish I did, but I —

STEPHEN. You ambushed me.

TOM. I have no idea what / you're —

STEPHEN. Ida's threatening to let the story out.

TOM. *What* story?

STEPHEN. That we met! That I fuckin' met with you!

TOM. How did she find out?

STEPHEN. Don't play dumb here, Tom.

TOM. You think *I* leaked it to her?

STEPHEN. Who else?

TOM. This isn't good, Steve.

STEPHEN. You're fucking right it isn't good.

TOM. I didn't leak it to her.

STEPHEN. Well I know *I* didn't, so that leaves you.

TOM. What's she know?

STEPHEN. She knows whatever you told her.

TOM. I swear I didn't leak it to her, Steve. I don't want this story out any more than you do.

STEPHEN. Too fucking late.

TOM. What did she tell you?

STEPHEN. She knows where and when we met. I don't think she knows anything else.

TOM. She has a source?

STEPHEN. Of course she has a source.

TOM. And you have no idea who it could be?

STEPHEN. Other than you?

TOM. Well it wasn't me, so it's gotta be someone else.

STEPHEN. Did you tell anyone? Anyone at all?

TOM. No. Did you?

STEPHEN. No.

TOM. Did you admit to meeting with me?

STEPHEN. No.

TOM. Then we stonewall her, and she's got nothing.

STEPHEN. She's gonna take the story to Drudge, or *Roll Call* — shit like that.

TOM. You can't stop her?

STEPHEN. She's trying to blackmail me — wants info about Thompson.

TOM. Then tell her what she wants to know.

STEPHEN. I can't do that.

TOM. You can't let this story get out.

STEPHEN. I'm not gonna be blackmailed, Tom.

TOM. You don't have much of a choice here.

STEPHEN. If I tell her about Thompson, I gotta tell her he's gonna endorse you guys.

TOM. Then tell her. I can handle it from my end if I start getting calls.

STEPHEN. No way. I told her we had Thompson in the bag. It'll make us look like fools.

TOM. You're gonna look like fools anyway when he endorses us.

STEPHEN. I can't do it, Tom. I can't let her blackmail me. I give in once, she'll do it again.

TOM. You're on a sinking ship, Steve. Tell her what she wants to know and jump. Come over to our side. We can control this thing. *(Pause. No answer from Stephen.)* Steve?

STEPHEN. I'm here.

TOM. Tell her about Thompson. Tell her you're coming over to us.

STEPHEN. I gotta go.

TOM. Listen to me —

STEPHEN. I really — …

TOM. Do the right thing here, Steve.

STEPHEN. I never should have met with you.

TOM. Get it together, kid. You and I can *control* this.

STEPHEN. I'm fucked, Tom.

TOM. No, you're not.

STEPHEN. Goodbye. *(Stephen hangs up.)*

TOM. Goddammit.

# Scene 2

*A small office at Morris' Iowa campaign headquarters. Molly is sitting at a desk, typing away at a laptop. Stephen enters the room abruptly.*

STEPHEN. Your phone's been off.

MOLLY. No, it hasn't. I / just don't —

STEPHEN. I've been trying to call you for the past three hours.

MOLLY. I don't get a good signal in this office.

STEPHEN. Did you talk to Ida Horowicz?

MOLLY. Ida? No.

STEPHEN. Don't lie to me.

MOLLY. I'm not. Why would I talk to Ida?

STEPHEN. Did you talk to anyone else?

MOLLY. Who? What are you talking about?

STEPHEN. Last night, when I was drunk, what did I tell you?

MOLLY. You told me about your girlfriend.

STEPHEN. What else?

MOLLY. Nothing. You talked about, Helen. That's it.

STEPHEN. I didn't tell you about a meeting?

MOLLY. No. You didn't tell me anything about a meeting.

STEPHEN. I didn't mention Tom Duffy?

MOLLY. Tom Duffy?

STEPHEN. If you're lying to me …

MOLLY. Steve. *What* is going on?

STEPHEN. I'm getting screwed is what's going on.

MOLLY. What happened?

STEPHEN. *(To himself.)* Who the fuck could it have been?

MOLLY. Could *what* have been?

STEPHEN. Someone told Ida, and I can't figure out who.

MOLLY. Told Ida *what?*

STEPHEN. Nothing.

MOLLY. You can trust me.

STEPHEN. You have no idea how fucked I am.

MOLLY. Will you *please* tell me what's going on?

STEPHEN. If I can just figure this out. I need to *think*.

MOLLY. I won't tell anyone Steve. Maybe I can help. *(A beat.)*

STEPHEN. Tom Duffy called me yesterday, right after we talked at the hotel. I met with him. He offered me a job on Pullman's campaign. I turned him down. But somehow Ida found out about the meeting. Duffy might have leaked it, but I don't think he did. And if you didn't, then I / don't know —

MOLLY. Even if you *had* told me I'd / never —

STEPHEN. I know, I know — but someone … fuck … *somebody* told Ida.

MOLLY. Where did you meet with him?

STEPHEN. A little restaurant in East Des Moines.

MOLLY. Was there anyone else there?

STEPHEN. Just us.

MOLLY. And you didn't tell anyone?

STEPHEN. No.

MOLLY. Then it has to be Duffy, right?

STEPHEN. Yeah, but I really don't think it's him. I just … If this thing gets out — this thing, it's like — if I had known. If I had any clue that —

MOLLY. You only *met* with him right?

STEPHEN. That's enough, believe me.

MOLLY. I don't see what the big deal is.

STEPHEN. It looks like backroom politicking — which is what it *was* I guess. Morris' press secretary meets with Pullman's campaign manager? The press'll eat it up. Am I jumping ship? Are we brokering a deal? It'll be a fucking feeding frenzy. I'll become the headline instead of the Governor. It'll drown out our message. And we can't afford it. Not with — not with all that's gonna happen in the next week. I mean — Molly — this race — it's — we're not gonna win this thing. Not Iowa at least. We're gonna have to scramble for every fucking vote in New Hampshire after we tank here, and we might / not be able to —

MOLLY. Hold on a sec. We're not gonna win Iowa?

STEPHEN. No.

MOLLY. But the polls say we're eight points —

STEPHEN. It's all a myth. We lost this state weeks ago. Everything you read, everything you hear, everything you see — it's all a myth. It's over. Iowa is fucking over already.

MOLLY. We're ahead …

STEPHEN. No. We're behind. The polls — they don't mean shit. And there's Thompson, and the robocalls and … Pullman's gonna take the state.

MOLLY. We *can't* lose.

STEPHEN. Wake the fuck up, Molly! I'm telling you this state is over and I *know.* You think you have any idea what's going on while you're sitting behind this fucking computer all day? Do you think you even have a shred of a clue?

MOLLY. Don't talk to me like that.

STEPHEN. I'm sorry. I am. It's just that — *(Stephen's phone rings. He looks at the number.)* Ida. *(Stephen looks at his watch.)* It's filing time.

MOLLY. Are you gonna answer it? *(The phone continues to ring.)*

STEPHEN. No. I'm not gonna answer it. *(The phone stops ringing.)* Well. That's that.

MOLLY. What's gonna happen?

STEPHEN. I don't know.

MOLLY. I'm sure you can — I mean — there's got to be a way to handle it, right?

STEPHEN. Maybe. I gotta talk to Paul. I gotta let Paul know what's gonna happen. Maybe if we — I don't know … *(Stephen opens the door.)*

MOLLY. Steve?

STEPHEN. Yeah?

MOLLY. I would never betray you like that.

STEPHEN. *(Not accusingly, but reflectively.)* I barely know you.

MOLLY. You just have to trust me.

STEPHEN. I'm not good at that. I want to trust you, but … It's just hard.

MOLLY. I'm not a reporter Stephen. I'm on your side.

STEPHEN. Why are you being so nice to me?

MOLLY. I don't know. Because I like you.

STEPHEN. You shouldn't like me Molly. I'm not a good person.

MOLLY. Well neither am I. So there. *(A brief pause while Stephen takes her in.)*

STEPHEN. Keep your cell phone on. *(Stephen exits.)*

## Scene 3

*A room in the Hotel Fort Des Moines. Paul is lying on the bed, talking on his cell phone.*

PAUL. Absolutely — there's no question about it ... *(A knock. Paul goes to the door, opens it and waves Stephen in, shutting the door behind him as he enters.)* But we've got to think broader strokes here, rethink everything ... Uh-huh ... Yeah, I know how to handle it ... Look, Stevie just got here. Can I call you back in a few minutes? ... Okay, bye. *(He hangs up.)* The Governor. We had a good long talk on the way back. He's up to speed with everything.
STEPHEN. How'd he take it?
PAUL. Better than I thought he would. Where've you been? I couldn't find you after the event.
STEPHEN. I left early. Drove straight back here. Wanted to start laying out a media plan for the next ten days.
PAUL. What do you have in mind?
STEPHEN. Well, assuming the worst, that we're gonna lose Iowa, I figure we need to downplay the state. We gear up the notion that we're running a national campaign. We stop stumping here altogether. Lower expectations. Start doing events in Super Tuesday states. That way when Pullman wins Iowa it's not as big of a blow. The media are prepared for it. And we've already started to shift the focus to Feb third.
PAUL. So you think we pull out of Iowa with just a week to go?
STEPHEN. I don't see any other choice.
PAUL. It's risky.
STEPHEN. But it'll lessen the blow. And if we come out of Iowa as the underdog, that might actually work for us. The Governor's a much better underdog than he is a front-runner. *(Paul goes over to the table and picks up some papers.)*
PAUL. You see this? *(He hands the papers to Stephen.)*
STEPHEN. What is it?
PAUL. Speech Ben wrote.
STEPHEN. He tried to give me a copy at the event, but I didn't

have time to look over it.

PAUL. I wanna use it. It's just what we need right now. The tone, the message. I think Iowans will really connect with it.

STEPHEN. Paul — I gotta tell you something.

PAUL. What's up?

STEPHEN. Ida knows I met with Duffy. *(Paul takes the speech out of Stephen's hands and places it back on the table.)* I'm sorry Paul. I don't know how she found out. Tried to blackmail me. Said she was gonna let the story out if I didn't tell her what happened at your meeting with Thompson.

PAUL. Did you tell her?

STEPHEN. Of course not. You know I wouldn't do that, Paul.

PAUL. So it's gonna hit the papers.

STEPHEN. Probably. Yeah. I figure she'll take it to Drudge or *Roll Call.* Whoever she takes it to, they'll have to call me for a comment, so I wanted to ask your advice here. I wanna know what you'd like me to say. I could just deny the whole thing, but if they call Duffy and he admits to it, that could look worse. If I say no comment they won't let up. Or, I could admit to it and try to spin it in a way that makes Duffy look bad. But I wanted to ask your advice first.

PAUL. I leaked it to Ida. *(Pause.)* At the event.

STEPHEN. What?

PAUL. We made a deal. She lets me read an advance copy of her profile, I give her a juicy little piece of gossip.

STEPHEN. I don't understand. Paul — this story's gonna hit the papers tomorrow morning.

PAUL. I know.

STEPHEN. But why? Why on earth would you do that to me? Why would you do that to the campaign.

PAUL. The campaign will survive.

STEPHEN. But what about me?

PAUL. Makes it easier to let you go.

STEPHEN. What?

PAUL. To let you *go,* Steve. To replace you.

STEPHEN. You're joking, right?

PAUL. No. I'm not.

STEPHEN. Don't do this, Paul.

PAUL. It's already done. The Governor knows. He agrees it's the right thing to do. I'm sorry Steve. Please don't take this personally.

STEPHEN. How the fuck am I not supposed to take this personally?

PAUL. Because it's politics.

STEPHEN. Paul —

PAUL. Why'd you meet with Duffy?

STEPHEN. I told you — I was confused. I wasn't thinking. I —

PAUL. Bullshit. You knew exactly what you were doing.

STEPHEN. It was a stupid mistake — okay? A very, very stupid mistake.

PAUL. No, Stephen. You didn't make a mistake. You made a choice. Yesterday — remember when you called me on the way to the airport? Remember that? "Hi Paul, this is Steve. I just got a — … " What? What did you just get? A call from Duffy? No. That's not what you told me. You stopped yourself. You *chose,* Stephen. You *chose* not to tell me. Why did you make that choice?

STEPHEN. I don't know …

PAUL. Sure you do. Because you were curious. Because you were flattered. Because it made you feel special to think Duffy wanted to speak to you instead of me. Because you thought to yourself: Maybe I can get something out of this. Because it made you feel *big.*

STEPHEN. That's not true, Paul. I don't know why I did what I did. But if you think it's because — because I wanted to prove something to myself, or because it somehow / made me feel — *(As he talks Paul takes out his wallet and pulls out a folded up dollar bill.)*

PAUL. *(Holding up the dollar bill.)* You know what this is? *(As he unfolds the bill.)* First campaign I ran — tiny little race in Kentucky — state senate seat. Workin' for a redneck nobody named Sam McGuthrie. Had no money, no staff, no fuckin' office. Worked out of McGuthrie's garage. Everyone thought we didn't stand a chance. But sure enough, we start to turn things around. Our numbers go up. Donations start trickling in. We hire a few people. Rent an office. Next thing you know, Sam looks like he's got a real chance. Incumbent is running scared. So what happens? State Republican Party doesn't want to lose this seat. They pour fifty grand into the other guy's coffers. Doesn't seem like a lot to us now, but in a small race like that, twenty years ago? It was a fortune. There's no way we can compete. Our party decides to abandon Sam. Didn't want to spend the money for a seat they thought they were gonna lose anyway. And about this time, a guy running a congressional campaign a few districts over gives me a call. Says, "I really like what you were able to do for poor ole Sam. But let's face it, he's a goner, so why don't you come work for me?" What do I do? Well Stephen — this is where you and I are different. I told Sam about the call. And Sam says to me, "Paul, you think this other guy's got a shot at winning, and he can pay you more than anything I can afford, so if it's what you feel you need to do, then I won't get in your way." So I say, "Sam — you took a chance and hired me when I was even more of nobody than you are, and I'll be damned if I'm gonna jump ship just because the shit hit the fan." We froze all the staff's salaries and poured every dime we had into winning the race. By election day I was literally down to one dollar in my pocket. This dollar. *(Beat.)* We lost the race, but three years later, when Sam decided to run for governor — who do you think he called? We *won* that race. And twenty years later — here I am. *(Beat.)* There's only one thing I value in this world, Steve, and that's loyalty. Without it, you're nothing and you have no one. And in politics it's the only currency that you can count on. That's why I'm letting you go. Not because you're not good enough. Hell, you're the best. But I value trust over talent. And I don't trust you anymore.

STEPHEN. What am I supposed to do?

PAUL. *(Placing the dollar bill back in his wallet.)* If I were you? I'd get a good night sleep. You're gonna get pounded by calls from the press in the morning.

STEPHEN. Who the fuck's gonna replace me?

PAUL. Ben.

STEPHEN. *Ben?*

PAUL. He's a smart kid. Not as good as you, but smart. And I trust him.

STEPHEN. He's fucking child.

PAUL. So are you.

STEPHEN. I built the press shop. From the ground up. No one knows the reporters better than I do. No one can run this thing like me. You can't just hand it over to Ben.

PAUL. Sure I can.

STEPHEN. I've worked my ass off for you Paul. I've fucking — I lost my girlfriend because of this campaign. I gave up a good job with Senator Callahan to do this. I —

PAUL. Wait wait wait. Am I supposed to feel *sorry* for you? Because you left Callahan? Because you got dumped by your *girlfriend?* You made your own bed, Stephen. You *made* those choices. If your girlfriend left you, it's because you wanted this job more than you wanted her. And even *her* you tried to spin, with that whole "open relationship" bullshit. And do you expect to be *rewarded* because you fucked up your personal life to come work for me? *(There's a knock on the door.)* IT'S OPEN. *(Ben enters, holding a few sheets of paper. He's surprised to see Stephen.)*

BEN. Steve. I didn't know you'd —

PAUL. Whattaya got, Ben?

BEN. That release you asked me to — ... The release you wanted to look over. *(Stephen grabs the release out of Ben's hands and looks at it.)*

STEPHEN. Irreconcilable differences? *(To Ben.)* Is that the best you could come up with?

PAUL. I told him to write that. And I suggest you say the same when the press calls you about it.

STEPHEN. You can go fuck yourself if you think that's what I'm gonna say.

PAUL. You can make this a soft landing, or make it hard on all of us. If I were you, I'd think down the road here. There will be other campaigns.

STEPHEN. This was the one, Paul.

PAUL. What do you want me to say?

STEPHEN. *(Turning on Ben.)* You little cunt. You've been waiting for this moment, haven't you? Writing your little speeches, schmoozing with the big boys.

BEN. No, Steve. It's not like that.

STEPHEN. You must be loving this.

PAUL. Get out, Steve.

STEPHEN. *(To Ben.)* I will take *so* much pleasure in watching you getting eaten alive.

PAUL. Leave, Stephen. *(Stephen hands Ben the crumpled up dollar bill.)*

STEPHEN. *(To Ben.)* Ask Paul to tell you the story about his buddy the redneck. It's a real tear-jerker. *(He begins to go. Stops and turns.)* And Paul — just so you know. Molly told me everything. I know you fucked her.

PAUL. Get the hell out of my room. *(Stephen exits, slamming the door behind him.)*

# Scene 4

*Later that evening. The same run-down restaurant where Stephen and Duffy met in Act One. Stephen is sitting at a table, nervously looking over a menu. Duffy enters.*

STEPHEN. Tom. Thanks for meeting with me.

TOM. I've only got a few minutes.

STEPHEN. I know. I'll keep it short. You want anything? A drink?

TOM. No. I'm fine.

STEPHEN. I'm gonna order a drink if you don't mind.

TOM. Course not. *(Stephen signals a waiter.)* So what's this about?

STEPHEN. I wanna come work for you.

TOM. I see.

STEPHEN. Is the offer still open?

TOM. A reporter at *Roll Call* phoned me this afternoon.

STEPHEN. I know who leaked it.

TOM. Who?

STEPHEN. Paul.

TOM. You told Paul?

STEPHEN. Yeah. I told him we met. He leaked it.

TOM. Why?

STEPHEN. He fired me, Tom. A few hours ago.

TOM. I'm sorry to hear that.

STEPHEN. Don't be. He's a — ... He's not who I thought he was. *(The waiter approaches.)*

WAITER. Anything to drink?

STEPHEN. I'll take a Dewar's on the rocks.

TOM. Just water for me. *(The waiter exits.)* You shouldn't have told him we met.

STEPHEN. I felt I had to.

TOM. So he fired you, and now you wanna come work for me.

STEPHEN. It's not like that. I was seriously thinking about working for you before any of this shit went down.

TOM. No you weren't.

STEPHEN. I was. Believe me. What you said yesterday. You're

right. I wanna work for a winner.

TOM.  You're saying that if Paul hadn't fired you we'd still be sitting here right now?

STEPHEN.  Yes.

TOM.  You're lying.

STEPHEN.  I'm not. I swear to God. I'll work my ass off for you, Tom.

TOM.  I'm sure you would.

STEPHEN.  And I can give you everything on Morris. *Everything.* I can lay out his whole strategy for you.

TOM.  I already know his strategy. Paul gave it all to Thompson.

STEPHEN.  I can give you the details. I can give you numbers. I can give you everything Thompson didn't.

TOM.  You'd do that to the Governor? To Paul?

STEPHEN.  They *dropped* me, Tom. They dropped my ass like I was yesterday's news. Yeah. I would.

TOM.  Revenge makes people unpredictable, Steve. I can't have someone who's unpredictable. Who's unstable.

STEPHEN.  *(Calmly.)* I'm not unstable.

TOM.  It's not just that / Steve.

STEPHEN.  I'm in control here. I'm on top / of things. I'm —

TOM.  Steve. Listen to me. This story in *Roll Call*, it's not good. I'm gonna start getting calls left and right. So are you. Then the networks will pick it up — the dailies …

STEPHEN.  It'll blow over. I can make that happen.

TOM.  I don't know if you can.

STEPHEN.  That's what I do. I make things blow over. I'm a pro at it. I can handle this story.

TOM.  If it had been a clean break — if you'd left Morris before this story broke, that'd be one thing. *That* we could control. But the way it'd look now — Paul fires you and *then* you come work for us. Looks like we're picking up the scraps. Puts Morris in the driver's seat. I can't have that.

STEPHEN.  You gotta hire me, Tom.

TOM.  I wish I could.

STEPHEN.  The Party needs me this cycle.

TOM.  Then go work for the DNC.

STEPHEN.  The *candidate* needs me.

TOM.  I think we'll be alright.

STEPHEN.  You practically begged me to work for you yesterday.

TOM. Things have changed.

STEPHEN. I'll work for next to nothing.

TOM. It's not a matter of money.

STEPHEN. Don't make me get on my knees here.

TOM. Steve — it's not gonna happen. I'm sorry. Go take a nice long vacation. You could use some time off. And maybe this thing is really a blessing in disguise. You're twenty-five. There's so many other things you could do besides this horseshit. Think about it. You make it to the White House. You do your four years, if you last that long, and then what? You get off the train every morning at Farragut North and trudge to some consulting firm with all the other political has-beens. Next thing you know you're forty, then fifty, so many races under your belt you can't remember which you won and which you lost. Do yourself a favor. Get out now. You stay in this business long enough you'll turn into nothing but a stone-hearted hack.

STEPHEN. Like you?

TOM. Yeah. Just like me.

STEPHEN. You played me, didn't you?

TOM. Played you? No. I tried to hire you.

STEPHEN. You knew I'd tell Paul.

TOM. I didn't *know.* I thought you *might,* but I didn't *know.*

STEPHEN. You knew if I told him he'd fire me.

TOM. Thing you gotta know about Paul — he's big on loyalty. *(Beat.)* Put yourself in my shoes, Steve. Your opponent has the best media mind in the country working on his team. What do you try to do? You either try to hire him yourself, or work it so if you can't have him, the other team can't either. This was a win-win situation for me. You work for us — great. Paul doesn't have you. Then again, if Paul fires you and I don't take you — fine — Paul still doesn't have you. The moment I got you to sit down in that chair yesterday, I knew I'd won. *(Tom stands.)* It's not *easy* for me to do this sort of thing, Steve. Don't think I take any pleasure in it. I'm sorry for you. I really am. Take care of yourself. *(Tom leaves. The waiter approaches with the drinks and sets them down on the table.)*

WAITER. Is your friend … Is he …

STEPHEN. He left.

WAITER. Just you then?

STEPHEN. Yeah.

WAITER. Ready to order? *(Stephen gulps down his drink.)*

59

STEPHEN. I'm not eating.

WAITER. Oh. Well maybe just an appetizer or something? The chicken quesadilla is really good.

STEPHEN. No. I'm not hungry.

WAITER. How about another drink?

STEPHEN. Just the check. *(The waiter clears his empty glass from the table. Starts to go. Stops and returns.)*

WAITER. I'm sorry to bother you, but you're that guy, right? From the Morris campaign? I've seen you on TV. Stephen Bentley, right?

STEPHEN. Bellamy.

WAITER. Right! Bellamy! Stephen Bellamy. I gotta say, I'm a big Morris supporter. Gonna caucus for him next week.

STEPHEN. Good for you.

WAITER. All these other guys, you can see right through them, but Morris, he's the real thing. I saw him speak when he came out here to East Des Moines a couple months ago.

STEPHEN. Yeah?

WAITER. Man — he really blew me away. That speech. Wow. That's really cool that you work for him. I'd give anything to work on a campaign like that.

STEPHEN. It's not as exciting as it looks.

WAITER. Still — to be right in there, right in the action. Making a real goddamn difference. You guys gotta win, you know. This country … *(He shakes his head.)* I mean don't get me wrong. My family — they made their way here a long time ago — just before I was born. And it's been good to us … but the last few years? It's like — my folks — they worked hard — saved up to open this place. They pay their taxes like everybody else — and what they got to show for it?

STEPHEN. You just said — they got this place.

WAITER. No — the *bank's* got this place. My brother — Miguel? Joins the marines a few years back. They send him overseas. A couple of weeks before he's supposed to come home … BAM. Right by the side of his truck. They wheel this vegetable off the plane. Can't speak, can't barely move — just sits there and blinks his eyes all day. We gotta mortgage this place to pay for his medical. I gotta work double shifts six days a week cuz my mama gotta be home takin' care of Miguel all the time. Just me and Pops keepin' this place open, and I don't know how much longer we can do that. *(Gestures around.)* Nobody ever here, even though we're cheap. We make it to next Christmas it'll be a miracle.

STEPHEN.  I'm sorry.

WAITER.  Don't be sorry, man. You just gotta win this election and set things straight. Hear what I'm sayin? *(Stephen just stares at him. The waiter smiles broadly.)* Let me get you another Dewar's. On the house. *(The waiter exits.)*

## Scene 5

*Stephen's room at the Hotel Fort Des Moines, later that night. Stephen is sitting in a chair, absently watching a basketball game on TV. He's got a gash on his head, and dried blood on his face. A knock. He puts the game on mute, listens. Another knock. Stephen goes to answer the door. He wobbles slightly as he walks. The muted TV continues to flicker throughout the scene.*

MOLLY.  Oh my God, what happened to you?

STEPHEN.  Nothing.

MOLLY.  You're bleeding.

STEPHEN.  I crashed my car.

MOLLY.  Jesus. Are you okay?

STEPHEN.  Where've you been?

MOLLY.  Let me see.

STEPHEN.  I'm *fine*. *(Molly takes a closer look at the gash.)*

MOLLY.  You need to see a doctor.

STEPHEN.  I'm not gonna see a doctor.

MOLLY.  You need stitches.

STEPHEN.  I've been calling you.

MOLLY.  Listen to me — you need —

STEPHEN.  No. I don't need stitches.

MOLLY.  *(Reaching toward his forehead.)* At least let me clean it out.

STEPHEN.  Leave it the fuck alone, okay?

MOLLY.  I'm just trying to help.

STEPHEN.  I don't want any help.

MOLLY.  What happened Steve? How'd you crash your car?

61

STEPHEN. Telephone pole.

MOLLY. You crashed into a telephone pole?

STEPHEN. Some kind of pole. I don't know. It was dark. And the snow. I don't know how I crashed it.

MOLLY. And they didn't take you to the hospital?

STEPHEN. Who?

MOLLY. The police?

STEPHEN. There were no police. I got out of the car and walked.

MOLLY. You just left the car there?

STEPHEN. Yeah. It had a pole in its engine.

MOLLY. Did you get knocked out?

STEPHEN. I don't remember.

MOLLY. You might have a concussion.

STEPHEN. It's just a little cut.

MOLLY. I really think we should go to the hospital.

STEPHEN. I'm not going anywhere.

MOLLY. You're drunk, aren't you?

STEPHEN. That would explain the pole, wouldn't it?

MOLLY. I'm calling an ambulance. *(She heads for the phone. Stephen knocks the phone off the nightstand before she can get to it.)*

STEPHEN. No you're not.

MOLLY. Alright look. You need to calm down and let me —

STEPHEN. Tell me where you've been.

MOLLY. I came as soon as I listened to your messages.

STEPHEN. I've been trying to reach you all night.

MOLLY. I was at dinner.

STEPHEN. With who?

MOLLY. No one.

STEPHEN. Who?

MOLLY. No one, I said.

STEPHEN. I don't believe you.

MOLLY. Paul. I was having dinner with Paul. *(Stephen laughs.)*

STEPHEN. That's just fucking fantastic.

MOLLY. You shouldn't have told him, Steve.

STEPHEN. The cocksucker deserved it.

MOLLY. You promised.

STEPHEN. Did you fuck him? After dinner?

MOLLY. Come on.

STEPHEN. Did you?

MOLLY. No!

STEPHEN. Did you want to?

MOLLY. I'm leaving. *(She starts to go.)*

STEPHEN. Molly …

MOLLY. I don't want to be around you when you're like this.

STEPHEN. Alright, alright …

MOLLY. You're being an asshole.

STEPHEN. You're right. I'm sorry.

MOLLY. That's not good enough.

STEPHEN. Please Molly … *(She eyes him. With complete humility and need:)* Please … Don't go … I'm asking … *(She takes a step closer.)*

MOLLY. Why'd you tell him?

STEPHEN. I was angry.

MOLLY. But I trusted you.

STEPHEN. You shouldn't have.

MOLLY. He fired me Steve.

STEPHEN. No …

MOLLY. He did. Right after he paid the check. He told me he never wanted to see me in the office again.

STEPHEN. That fucking prick.

MOLLY. You got me fired.

STEPHEN. Well I got fired too. So I guess that makes two of us.

MOLLY. Are you hearing me? I got fired because of *you.*

STEPHEN. Alright. Here's the plan. You go to Paul and you tell 'im that if he doesn't give your job back you're gonna call every newspaper in the country and say that —

MOLLY. Are you crazy?

STEPHEN. It'll work. Believe me.

MOLLY. No. I'm not gonna do that.

STEPHEN. You gotta hit this fucker back.

MOLLY. No I don't.

STEPHEN. Why are you protecting him?

MOLLY. I'm not. I'm protecting myself.

STEPHEN. If you want your job back this is what you gotta do.

MOLLY. I *don't* want my job back.

STEPHEN. Molly.

MOLLY. You don't care about me getting my job back. You just want to use me to get back at Paul.

STEPHEN. That's not true.

MOLLY. You're just like him …

STEPHEN. Who? Paul?

MOLLY. This isn't some *game,* Stephen.

STEPHEN. You don't know me.

MOLLY. You know what. This is pointless …

STEPHEN. I'll tell you about me. Do you want to hear?

MOLLY. Look …

STEPHEN. You wanna feel sorry for yourself?

MOLLY. No. I —

STEPHEN. You didn't lose a job. You lost an *internship.* A fucking *internship.* I'm the one who lost the job, okay? I'm the one who —

MOLLY. Steve …

STEPHEN. Guess what I've been doing for the last five hours …

MOLLY. Stop it …

STEPHEN. I met with Duffy again. I practically begged him to hire me. But he said no. Straight to my face, like I was nothing. Then I listened to some waiter tell me how his brother's brain got chopped into mince-meat overseas. How his family was gonna lose their restaurant, have to go back to Mexico, on and on and on. That's what I was doing while you were having dinner with Paul. Listening to this guy's sob story for an hour while he forced drinks down my throat.

MOLLY. You were *probably* thinking what a good story this waiter's brother would make if you got him up on the stage with Morris. All the great articles flashed / before your eyes. You probably didn't even —

STEPHEN. It *would* have made a great story. Yes. If I could get him on stage with Morris, it'd be fucking golden. Dude in a wheelchair drooling onto his shirt while the Governor placed a hand on his shoulder and told the world he was gonna fix everything. But you know what? I don't *work* for the Governor anymore, so it doesn't matter how good this guy's story was. His story doesn't mean shit. Because it'll never see the light of day.

MOLLY. You know what? Getting fired is probably the best thing that'll ever happen to you.

STEPHEN. I'm getting pretty fuckin' tired of people saying what's good for me.

MOLLY. You're like a — I don't what you are …

STEPHEN. You want me to say I'm a monster? That I have no soul? That I —

MOLLY. All I'm saying is —

STEPHEN. Fine. I'm a monster. I'm a fucking horror show. A

fucking loser and a fucking idiot and a fucking —

MOLLY. Stop it Steve.

STEPHEN. Why? Why should I stop? I've come this far in ruining my life. Why stop now?

MOLLY. You haven't ruined your life …

STEPHEN. What do I have to fall back on? My girlfriend who dumped me because I'm never home? Some bullshit consulting job in D.C.? I'd suffocate. I've been working in politics since I was fifteen years old. Ten years. Without it I don't —

MOLLY. Sit down.

STEPHEN. I don't wanna sit —

MOLLY. SIT THE FUCK DOWN. *(Stephen is taken aback by her forcefulness. He stops. Quieter now:)* Come on. Sit right here. *(Stephen sits on the edge of the bed. Molly grabs a pillow and pulls the casing off.)*

STEPHEN. What are you doing?

MOLLY. Be quiet. *(She starts to dab at the cut on Stephen's forehead. He winces and pulls back.)*

STEPHEN. Oww.

MOLLY. Let me do this. *(She continues to clean the wound as Stephen grimaces. A moment passes.)*

STEPHEN. Why did you sleep with Paul?

MOLLY. I don't wanna talk about it.

STEPHEN. Please?

MOLLY. Be still.

STEPHEN. How did it happen?

MOLLY. Enough talking, okay?

STEPHEN. I need to know. *(Molly takes a tired sigh. Decides to give in and tell him if it will keep him calm.)*

MOLLY. Because I was stupid. Because it made me feel special and I fell for it. He kept telling me how smart I was. How *mature* I was. How talented. And it felt good to hear that. To get that kind of attention. Half of me knew he was lying, but the other half wanted to believe him. So I decided to let myself. To believe him. Then one night, we were in his office and he shut the door and he … anyway …

STEPHEN. Was it the same with me?

MOLLY. Was what?

STEPHEN. Did you think I was lying to you? The things I said?

MOLLY. I didn't care. *(She finishes cleaning the wound.)* There. That's a little better.

STEPHEN. I wasn't lying to you.

MOLLY. It doesn't matter now anyway.

STEPHEN. But I wasn't.

MOLLY. Fine.

STEPHEN. It's important to me that you know that.

MOLLY. Well now I know. Let's get you to a doctor.

STEPHEN. Can we just stay here?

MOLLY. You really need stitches.

STEPHEN. What's wrong with me?

MOLLY. You have a bad cut, that's all.

STEPHEN. No — I mean what's *wrong* with me?

MOLLY. Nothing's wrong with you. Come on. Let's get outta here.

STEPHEN. There has to be something wrong. Otherwise this wouldn't have happened. I wouldn't be sitting here right now bleeding like this — I'd still have my job. I'd be —

MOLLY. Will you forget about your job for a second?

STEPHEN. What am I gonna do, Molly?

MOLLY. I don't know. You can figure that out tomorrow.

STEPHEN. I'm nothing without this job.

MOLLY. There are other things in the world besides politics.

STEPHEN. Not to me.

MOLLY. Well that's what's wrong with you then.

STEPHEN. But I don't ... I don't know anything else. I don't even know where to begin.

MOLLY. It's okay Steve. You're gonna be fine.

STEPHEN. Can you describe it to me?

MOLLY. No I can't. You get to start over.

STEPHEN. How? How do I do that?

MOLLY. I can't answer all these questions for you.

STEPHEN. You're making me ask them — so help me answer them.

MOLLY. I'm not making you do anything. I'm just trying to get you to a hospital.

STEPHEN. You think you're some kind of saint, don't you?

MOLLY. *What?*

STEPHEN. You get to come to the rescue ... pick up all the pieces. *(Suddenly cold.)* You know what? Fuck this.

MOLLY. Steve.

STEPHEN. No. Fuck all of this. This is bullshit is what it is. This is ... I don't deserve this. This isn't who I am ... Feeling sorry for myself. Acting like a goddamn pussy. I don't lose — I win. Even when I lose I win. I'm not gonna let Paul or Duffy or you, or *anyone* — no way — not a chance …

MOLLY. Grow up, Stephen!

STEPHEN. *Grow up?* And how the fuck old are you are?

MOLLY. It has nothing to do with —

STEPHEN. The fact that you're a teenager? That you're fucking *nineteen*? Yeah. I think it does. What fucking right do you have telling me to grow up?

MOLLY. Jesus Christ …

STEPHEN. You don't know who I am. But you wanna know who *you* are? Because I can tell you … You're that cute little girl, the one with a couple more brain cells than all the others, prancing around, sniffing out the big dogs like a bitch in heat. Because it makes you feel good that somebody with actual power will take ten minutes out of their schedule to bend you over in a closet.

MOLLY. Goodbye Steve. *(She makes for the door. Stephen grabs her handbag. Heads to the other side of the room.)* Give it back.

STEPHEN. *(Rooting around in the bag.)* Where's your phone?

MOLLY. I said give it back. *(Stephen finds the phone.)* Use your own fucking phone.

STEPHEN. I think this might be better coming from yours. *(Stephen starts to dial, holds the phone to his ear.)*

MOLLY. *(Getting alarmed.)* Who're you calling?

STEPHEN. Who do you think?

MOLLY. I'm gonna go get someone. *(She heads for the door again. As she opens it.)*

STEPHEN. Hello Ida? It's Steve. I've got a story for you … *(Molly stops dead in her tracks.)*

MOLLY. Don't …

STEPHEN. No — It's about Paul. *(Molly lunges for the phone.)* Hold on a sec … *(He throws her to the bed. Puts the phone to his chest with one hand, warns Molly with the other.)* Calm down.

MOLLY. Please don't do this … *(She realizes there's no use fighting him. He puts the phone back to his ear.)*

STEPHEN. Sorry about that — it was the *cleaning lady. (Molly watches him, paralyzed.)* So the story — this is a good one Ida. And if I give you this story, you're gonna do a feature on me — my version of the last couple days —and you're gonna find a way to get it in the *Times.* You ready? *(Stephen stares right at her as he says the following.)*

Paul had an affair with a nineteen-year-old intern … That's right — nineteen years old. Her name is Molly Pearson. P-E-A-R-S-O-N. This phone I'm calling you from? It's hers. Call her. And if she won't talk, you can cite me as a source. I'll tell you everything … Right now if you want. I'll meet you at the bar downstairs in ten. *(He flips the phone shut. Stares icily at Molly. She's frozen, clearly devastated. Stephen puts on his sports coat. Straightens his tie, smoothes his hair.)* You should come down with me. You can give her your side of the story.

MOLLY. How could you do that?

STEPHEN. How could I not? *(He makes his way to the door. Then turns back to her.)* You coming with or staying behind? *(But she just stares at him. The scene freezes in tableau. A burst of camera flashes. Ben appears in a pin spot. Stephen and Molly remain frozen in silhouette. Ben addresses the audience as though they were a press pool. He has the confidence, polish and self-possession we saw Stephen exhibit at the beginning of the play.)*

BEN. For those of you who don't know me, my name is Benjamin Fowles. I'll be taking over as the Governor's new communications director. The Governor has this statement to make … *(He reads from a piece of paper.)* "Paul Zara and Stephen Bellamy served our campaign well from day one. While we regret the circumstances under which they must leave us, we will always be grateful for the contributions both have made in getting us a few steps closer to the White House." *(Ben now looks up and addresses the audience directly. He knows this part by heart. He should — because he wrote it.)* This election is not about who and who doesn't work for *us*, but how we can work for *you* — the American people. It's *your* best interests which should be making headlines, not minor shake-ups in our organization. Rest assured that this small bump in the road will not deter us — we're strong as ever and getting stronger by the day. Because we get our strength from *you* — from *your* hard work, *your* dedication, *your* belief that we can make this country a better place for us all. And as long as you keep giving us *your* strength, we'll deliver you the stronger, safer America you all deserve. *(Beat.)* Thank you very much. I won't be taking questions. *(Blackout.)*

## End of Play

# PROPERTY LIST

Drinks
Roll-away suitcase
Wristwatch
Engagement ring
Chewing tobacco
Cash
Car keys
Manila envelope with papers
Cell phone
Jacket, pen, napkin
Briefcase with folder and papers
Clothing
Newspapers
Sheets of paper
Laptop
Dollar bill
Phone
Pillow, pillow case
Handbag with cell phone in it

# SOUND EFFECTS

Cell phone ring
Muffled cheers
Massive cheer

# NEW PLAYS

★ **AT HOME AT THE ZOO by Edward Albee.** Edward Albee delves deeper into his play THE ZOO STORY by adding a first act, HOMELIFE, which precedes Peter's fateful meeting with Jerry on a park bench in Central Park. "An essential and heartening experience." –*NY Times.* "Darkly comic and thrilling." –*Time Out.* "Genuinely fascinating." –*Journal News.* [2M, 1W] ISBN: 978-0-8222-2317-7

★ **PASSING STRANGE book and lyrics by Stew, music by Stew and Heidi Rodewald, created in collaboration with Annie Dorsen.** A daring musical about a young bohemian that takes you from black middle-class America to Amsterdam, Berlin and beyond on a journey towards personal and artistic authenticity. "Fresh, exuberant, bracingly inventive, bitingly funny, and full of heart." –*NY Times.* "The freshest musical in town!" –*Wall Street Journal.* "Excellent songs and a vulnerable heart." –*Variety.* [4M, 3W] ISBN: 978-0-8222-2400-6

★ **REASONS TO BE PRETTY by Neil LaBute.** Greg really, truly adores his girlfriend, Steph. Unfortunately, he also thinks she has a few physical imperfections, and when he mentions them, all hell breaks loose. "Tight, tense and emotionally true." –*Time Magazine.* "Lively and compulsively watchable." –*The Record.* [2M, 2W] ISBN: 978-0-8222-2394-8

★ **OPUS by Michael Hollinger.** With only a few days to rehearse a grueling Beethoven masterpiece, a world-class string quartet struggles to prepare their highest-profile performance ever—a televised ceremony at the White House. "Intimate, intense and profoundly moving." –*Time Out.* "Worthy of scores of bravissimos." –*BroadwayWorld.com.* [4M, 1W] ISBN: 978-0-8222-2363-4

★ **BECKY SHAW by Gina Gionfriddo.** When an evening calculated to bring happiness takes a dark turn, crisis and comedy ensue in this wickedly funny play that asks what we owe the people we love and the strangers who land on our doorstep. "As engrossing as it is ferociously funny." –*NY Times.* "Gionfriddo is some kind of genius." –*Variety.* [2M, 3W] ISBN: 978-0-8222-2402-0

★ **KICKING A DEAD HORSE by Sam Shepard.** Hobart Struther's horse has just dropped dead. In an eighty-minute monologue, he discusses what path brought him here in the first place, the fate of his marriage, his career, politics and eventually the nature of the universe. "Deeply instinctual and intuitive." –*NY Times.* "The brilliance is in the infinite reverberations Shepard extracts from his simple metaphor." –*TheaterMania.* [1M, 1W] ISBN: 978-0-8222-2336-8

DRAMATISTS PLAY SERVICE, INC.
440 Park Avenue South, New York, NY 10016 212-683-8960 Fax 212-213-1539
postmaster@dramatists.com  www.dramatists.com

# NEW PLAYS

★ **AUGUST: OSAGE COUNTY by Tracy Letts.** WINNER OF THE 2008 PULITZER PRIZE AND TONY AWARD. When the large Weston family reunites after Dad disappears, their Oklahoma homestead explodes in a maelstrom of repressed truths and unsettling secrets. "Fiercely funny and bitingly sad." –*NY Times.* "Ferociously entertaining." –*Variety.* "A hugely ambitious, highly combustible saga." –*NY Daily News.* [6M, 7W] ISBN: 978-0-8222-2300-9

★ **RUINED by Lynn Nottage.** WINNER OF THE 2009 PULITZER PRIZE. Set in a small mining town in Democratic Republic of Congo, RUINED is a haunting, probing work about the resilience of the human spirit during times of war. "A full-immersion drama of shocking complexity and moral ambiguity." –*Variety.* "Sincere, passionate, courageous." –*Chicago Tribune.* [8M, 4W] ISBN: 978-0-8222-2390-0

★ **GOD OF CARNAGE by Yasmina Reza, translated by Christopher Hampton.** WINNER OF THE 2009 TONY AWARD. A playground altercation between boys brings together their Brooklyn parents, leaving the couples in tatters as the rum flows and tensions explode. "Satisfyingly primitive entertainment." –*NY Times.* "Elegant, acerbic, entertainingly fueled on pure bile." –*Variety.* [2M, 2W] ISBN: 978-0-8222-2399-3

★ **THE SEAFARER by Conor McPherson.** Sharky has returned to Dublin to look after his irascible, aging brother. Old drinking buddies Ivan and Nicky are holed up at the house too, hoping to play some cards. But with the arrival of a stranger from the distant past, the stakes are raised ever higher. "Dark and enthralling Christmas fable." –*NY Times.* "A timeless classic." –*Hollywood Reporter.* [5M] ISBN: 978-0-8222-2284-2

★ **THE NEW CENTURY by Paul Rudnick.** When the playwright is Paul Rudnick, expectations are geared for a play both hilarious and smart, and this provocative and outrageous comedy is no exception. "The one-liners fly like rockets." –*NY Times.* "The funniest playwright around." –*Journal News.* [2M, 3W] ISBN: 978-0-8222-2315-3

★ **SHIPWRECKED! AN ENTERTAINMENT—THE AMAZING ADVENTURES OF LOUIS DE ROUGEMONT (AS TOLD BY HIMSELF) by Donald Margulies.** The amazing story of bravery, survival and celebrity that left nineteenth-century England spellbound. Dare to be whisked away. "A deft, literate narrative." –*LA Times.* "Springs to life like a theatrical pop-up book." –*NY Times.* [2M, 1W] ISBN: 978-0-8222-2341-2

**DRAMATISTS PLAY SERVICE, INC.**
440 Park Avenue South, New York, NY 10016  212-683-8960  Fax 212-213-1539
*postmaster@dramatists.com*  *www.dramatists.com*